SELLING YOUR HOME
For **TOP DOLLAR**

17 VALUABLE TIPS FROM TOP REAL ESTATE AGENTS FOR GETTING YOUR HOME SOLD FAST AND AT YOUR PRICE

RUDY L. KUSUMA

SELLING YOUR HOME
For TOP DOLLAR

RUDY L. KUSUMA

© 2015 Rudy L. Kusuma

All rights reserved. No portion of this book may be reproduced, stored in a retrieval system, or transmitted in any form or by any means - electronic, mechanical, photocopy, recording, scanning, or any other - except for brief quotations in critical reviews or articles, without the prior written permission of the publisher.

Every effort has been made to obtain permissions for material quoted throughout the book. If any required acknowledgments have been omitted, or any rights overlooked, it is unintentional. Please notify the publisher of any omission, and it will be rectified in future editions.

Cover design and interior formatting / typesetting by William Reynolds

Printed in the United States

CONTENTS

Foreword by Rudy L. Kusuma		6
ONE	Selling Your Home In The 21st Century by Myranda Shields	9
TWO	Hiring For Reputation by Sandy Casella	13
THREE	Ways To Properly Set Up Your Listing by Sandy Casella	15
FOUR	Pricing Is Part Of The 4 P's by Myranda Shields	19
FIVE	Don't Buy A House Without Your Agent by Sandy Casella	23
SIX	The Power Of Multiple Listing Service (MLS) by John Gluch	27
SEVEN	Leverage The Power Of Social Media by Jonathan Lahey	31
EIGHT	Creating Value From The Inside Out by Rudy L. Kusuma	35
NINE	Staging To Sell by Ahmad Shalforoshzadeh	39
TEN	The Investment And Second Home Seller by Jared W. Jones	47
ELEVEN	Buying And Selling Equestrian Estates by Kirstin Kutchuk	57
TWELVE	Buyer Profile Systems by Sarah Grimm	65
THIRTEEN	Contracts by Adam Kutchuk	69
FOURTEEN	Don't Sell Your House More Than Once by John Gluch	73
FIFTEEN	How To Write Classefied Ads That Sell Homes by Ahmad Shalforoshzadeh	81
SIXTEEN	Marketing: Internet Based Effectiveness by Nancy Braun	87
SEVENTEEN	Blogging And Content Marketing Strategy by Nancy Braun	91
About The Authors		94

Foreword

By Rudy L. Kusuma

If only selling a property were as simple as placing a for sale sign in the yard and making an appointment with the closing company to sign the paperwork. Unfortunately, there are many pitfalls in the process of buying and selling real estate that should be avoided if at all possible.

Do I Absolutely Need A Realtor?

Real estate professionals only make a commission when a property is sold; they don't work for an hourly wage. Therefore, it is important for a real estate agent to be good with business planning, time management, budgeting and marketing in order to be successful in the real estate industry. Furthermore, the vast majority of realtors are independent contractors, meaning they are responsible for everything about their business including taxes and choosing which brokerage with which to hang their license.

Selecting an Agent

Many sellers make common mistakes when it comes to selecting a real estate agent. Pricing their property and staging/marketing are among the top of the list of mistakes. This book will further outline a variety of common pitfalls that sellers make and tips on how to sell your home for top dollar. Top real estate professionals from around the United States and Canada have all contributed to writing about top lessons learned for buying and selling. Among the top attributes that buyers and sellers look for in real estate agents are negotiation skills, marketing techniques, business ethics, understanding the property and the client, as well as being familiar with the neighborhood in which the property resides.

It is estimated that there are currently 2 million active real estate licensees in the United States alone. According to the National Association of Realtors 5,090,000 existing homes were sold in 2013 alone, this roughly equates to an average of 13,945 homes sold each and every day if we are to include weekends and holidays. Throw technology and social media into the real estate mix, and the ways homes are bought and sold have changed dramatically over the past decade.

While some homeowners undertake selling their own home through listing it as a For Sale By Owner (FSBO), this population only roughly accounts for 9% of all home sellers according to 2013 statistics. What's more is that sales prices are substantially lower for FSBO homes, In 2013, the typical FSBO home sold for $184,000 compared to a $230,000 price tag for an agent-assisted home sale. That's a difference of $46,000 and a lot of time lost on your behalf handling the sale of your home. After you have read and re-read this statistic how can you afford not to use an agent for the sale of your home?

Selling a home can be complicated. The good news is real estate professionals have years of experience under their belt to better help you understand the correct way to prepare your home for the market, proper pricing strategy, handling of contracts and negotiation.

Real estate is the largest personal asset that one will most likely ever hold. Decisions surrounding the buying and selling of a property are not to be taken lightly. This book was written as a way to coach buyers, sellers and real estate agents through the complicated processes of real estate. It is my sincere hope that you pick up some sound advice through reading the following pages and are able to put it to good use in your next real estate transaction.

> You open yourself up to a lot of liabilities and potentially harmful situations by not having somebody experienced to oversee things for you.

ONE

Selling Your Home In The 21st Century

By Myranda Shields

There are a variety of ways to sell your home. The most common way, and the way with the least amount of liability and stress, is to hire a real estate agent and have him/her list the home for you on the local Multiple Listing Service (MLS). This is a system that is used by realtors across the country to communicate with each other about the homes they have available. The best way to get your home in front of buyers is to get it in front of the agents that are regularly working with the buyers. The MLS does this. The real estate world has become quite advanced, and these days having the property in the MLS not only means having it where the real estate agents search, it also means having it syndicated to dozens of other sites that attract possible buyers. This is only one of the benefits of using a realtor to sell your home.

The home selling/buying process is a stressful one. There are so many moving parts; it is a lot of work to make sure that everybody is doing their proper jobs in the proper time frames while you are simultaneously packing everything you own, living out of boxes, and still dealing with life's other demands. Using an agent helps mitigate this stress by giving you one point of contact; one person to communicate with that cares about you and the needs of your family. The realtor will negotiate the best possible offer on your behalf. They will give you different options and help you weigh your pros and cons. They are aware of the pitfalls of different scenarios, and they have the experience to guide you through the ups and downs that come along with selling the home you love. There are a lot of liabilities that go along with selling a home when you use an agent; they bear a lot of the liability for you and make sure that you take certain steps to reduce your liability as much as you possibly can.

A realtor isn't necessary to sell your home. You can sell your home yourself the same way you would sell anything else you own. A lot of websites offer free ways to market your home to potential buyers, and you can take out a classified ad, and put a sign in front of your home asking potential buyers to call you. In theory it sounds like a good idea. You can save money on commissions and get the same result, right? This is a risky strategy similar to being in legal trouble and representing yourself instead of hiring an attorney. Just because you can do it, doesn't mean it is a good idea. You open yourself up to a lot of liabilities and potentially harmful situations by not having somebody experienced to oversee things for you. You wouldn't just post your phone number out in front of your house encouraging people to come look through your personal belongings. That is exactly what you are doing when you try to sell your home without using a real estate agent. You have no way of gauging the legitimacy of buyers. A person could lead you to believe they are interested in purchasing your home and have purely a criminal intent that could endanger your family. If you only allow buyers that have real estate agents with them into your home you know that they are legitimate buyers and not just there to get an idea of where you hide your valuables. The agent must accompany them the entire time.

When selling your home by yourself, you are also responsible for writing contracts and disclosures. You can find editable forms online and fill in the blanks. Selling a home is a high dollar and complex transaction. Not knowing how to protect yourself by disclosing the right things at the right times and knowing every option available to you if something doesn't go according to plan is very risky. If the buyer is getting a loan, the lender will require the seller to sign certain documents and may even require a specified state contract be used. When this happens, the buyer has professionals looking out for their best interest, requiring the seller to sign forms that protect the buyer. Who is protecting the seller? The seller, and unless the seller has a lot of real estate and/or legal experience, this can end horribly. Typically, sellers don't save very much money over using an experienced and qualified agent. Most of the time, when weighing pros and cons, you'll find the risk and stress of selling a home yourself isn't worth the small reward.

Another way to sell your home that recently has increased in popularity is via online auction sites such as eBay. There are some other auction sites that are only available in specific states, and many of require you have multiple listings. eBay does not have this requirement. Your real estate agent can list your property on an auction site, and this can be done at the same time as the MLS listing. Using an auction site helps to promote your property to buyers who reside in different states. Auction sites are ideal for people who sell properties that are appealing to investors or somebody looking for vacation homes. Many times homebuyers looking to live in the home are put off by the uncertainties of auctions since many of them remove or limit the inspection period. If you think an auction may be ideal for your home, discuss the options with your agent who will be familiar with the different auction sites in your area.

Your agent can then tell you what their track record looks like compared to the average. Is it better, worse or the same?

TWO

Hiring for Reputation

By Sandy Casella

How do you plan to hire your next Real Estate Agent? This may depend on whether you are buying a home, selling a home or doing both. One study from the National Association of Realtors showed that only 65% of sellers would use the same agent again. A number of reasons are cited, but the number one reason is poor communication. Why does this happen and what can you do about it when you choose your next real estate agent?

A few facts to consider:

- The typical home seller in 2013 was 53 years of age, had a median household income of $97,500, and lived in their home for 9 years.

- 88% of sellers were assisted by a real estate agent when selling their home.

- Recent sellers typically sold their homes for 97% of the listing price, and 47% reported reducing the asking price at least once.

- The typical home sold was on the market for 5 weeks.

- 39% of sellers used a real estate agent found through a referral by friends or family.

- 25% used the agent they previously worked with to buy or sell a home.

There are a number of ways in which you may choose your next agent: a referral from a friend or relative, an agent you meet at an open house you attend, an agent you meet because you are responding to an ad in the newspaper, or perhaps you feel obligated to use a friend or family member even though you believe they may or may not be the best person for the job. Which is the best way to find and hire your next agent?

How about hiring a person based on their reputation? This takes a number of different forms, but it certainly does not mean the agent who takes out the biggest ad in the newspaper. This is not reputation; this is dollars spent.

When it comes time to hire an agent to represent you, you need to know what their track record is and what other people have experienced working with them

How do you find out what other buyers and sellers have to say about a particular realtor? How do you find out what that Realtors track record is? Simply ask them. Ask them to show you statistics for your area on how many homes are for sale, how many went for sale and how many actually sold. What was the average list to sales price ratio? How many days were those homes actually on the market?

Your agent can then tell you what their track record looks like compared to the average. Is it better, worse or the same?

How about what others have said about your realtor? Can they produce testimonials from some of their clients that tell the story of what they were able to accomplish for them? Were they able to get their home sold for them in a reasonable amount of time? Were they able to get them more than the average price for the area?

One of the biggest mistakes you can make when you sell your home is choose an agent based on what they said they can get you for your home. What that agent says adds no value to your home. There are countless stories of people whose homes sit on the market day after day, week after week and yes even month after month because they chose an agent based on a high sale price. Even in a very fast paced market not every home sells and all markets are particularly price sensitive. Buyers are very educated; they have a lot of information at their fingertips, and they know what homes are worth.

Hiring your agent based on price will lead to disappointment. Imagine having that agent come back thirty days later to tell you that your home is overpriced, and now you have to reduce it. Or worse yet, not coming back thirty days later. Envision yourself having to chase your realtor down to find out why you don't have any offers, and why you don't have anyone coming to see your house?

Hire your agent based on reputation and you won't suffer these frustrations.

THREE

Ways To Properly Set Up Your Listing

By Sandy Casella

So you have decided it's time to sell your home. You have done your research on other properties for sale in your neighborhood. You have a fairly good idea of where you want to go, and have chosen someone to help you sell it. Now you need to get your home ready to market to the public.

Whether this is your family home or an investment property, setting up your listing to attract buyers is extremely important. This is the 'launch' of a very valuable asset - your home. Don't underestimate the importance of setting up your listing.

Custom Marketing Plan

Once you have decided which real estate agent you are going to hire, a custom marketing plan should be prepared by the agent, The plan will spell out how your home will be marketed to the public. Every home is different and every home needs to be marketed differently to attract the most traffic. Discuss with your real estate agent how they plan to attract buyers. Does your agent have buyers they are currently working with that would be potentially interested? Does he/she know the type of buyer that will be attracted to your home?

Ads and Sales Sheets

Ads and sales sheets need to be prepared. These must be written to hit the buyer's hot buttons and compel them to want more information. The details need to be non-eliminating. Your agent should know how to write compelling content that will cause a buyer to seek out more information about your house. Words like, quiet, tree-lined street, are more likely to hit their emotional hot button, and compel them to ask more questions. Your realtor's network of co-operative agents and real estate investors should be alerted to the listing. Most importantly, a sales sheet should be sent to your realtor's list of buyers in waiting. This is their own personal list of buyers who've registered information pertaining to types of homes they would like to buy. Your agent may be able to sell the home just by matching it with one of their buyers.

Aggressive Marketing

In order for your home to create a high level of demand, an aggressive marketing plan needs to be put in place including listing your home on your local MLS (Multiple Listing Service) and all surrounding MLS systems that attract buyers. Also, you home should be listed on Realtor.com, all of your agent's websites, all of the public websites, local newspapers sites, etc. There are countless websites where your home can be featured.

Signage

Buyers will drive the neighborhood they are looking in to see if there are any homes they like, so make sure your signage is set up to draw them in. A good realtor will have prominent signage on your lawn that is not just a for sale sign but an attention getter as well. Buyers typically drive through a neighborhood, write down a bunch of phone numbers and addresses with very good intentions of getting in touch with every agent who's sign they saw. They quickly come to realize that it is not all that easy to get in touch with some of them. They either don't get a call back or they can't remember which house they saw where. They may play telephone tag so long they eventually give up. A good sign will offer them an easy way to get the information they want about your home. It's no secret that if you make it easy for the prospect to get the information they want, you will create more demand.

Guaranteed Sale

Some real estate agents will guarantee the sale of your home. This can take on a number of forms. They may guarantee that they will buy your home if they don't sell it. They may give you a guaranteed price for your home, and if they don't sell it for the agreed on price they will pay you the difference. If your agent will guarantee the sale of your buyer's home, you will attract a larger pool of buyers. The majority of buyers, 80%, will have a home that they need to sell before they can buy yours. Guaranteeing the sale of the buyer's home means that buyer can buy your home with no strings attached, resulting in a faster sale for you.

Pictures

We all know a picture is worth a thousand words, right? It's important that you have good quality photos of your home and have as many on the listing as possible. Most real estate boards have a limit on the number of pictures that can be added to a listing. Whatever that number is try to use it up. The pictures should be bright and show as many key aspects of the home as possible. Do not let the listing go live without the pictures. This is extremely important, even the most eager buyers will forget to go back to see if pictures have been posted causing you to lose ready to act buyers.

Creating Demand

Creating demand for your home will result in more money in your pocket. Make sure that you choose an agent that can demonstrate how they will create that demand, and don't choose the agent based on what they say they can get for your home. They need to show you by demonstrating how they have done it in the past for other clients.

Your real estate agent can get statistics on your neighborhood and your entire market, and goals on traffic (showings of your home) should be set in advance.

FOUR

Pricing is Part Of The 4 P's

By Myranda Shields

Selling a house is an emotional process. It isn't just a house, it is a home; it's the place that you made memories with your family. It is very hard for people to separate themselves from the emotions that come up when making the decision to part with the place that you have looked forward to coming home to for so many years. However, in most life situations, when emotions get in the way of logic things can get more complicated than they need to be. This is also true in the case of selling the family home. It needs to be looked at the same way one would look at selling a car or anything else that you would sell to an end user who isn't looking to purchase a brand new product.

When marketing executives for big companies are looking to put a product on the market, they look at the marketing mix. The marketing mix consists of different features of marketing and how they will work together to maximize profit and reduce time in inventory. The marketing mix consists of the 4 P's of marketing which are: Price, Product, Place and Promotion. Many times people don't consider all of these when deciding how to sell their family home. Most of the time, they think "I love this home, I have spent so much time and money making this home perfect. I can just have any agent throw it in the MLS, and the buyers will flock in to give me what I want for it. I know the value is there." Typically, this scenario is not the case. A well thought out marketing plan needs to be put together and flawlessly executed in order to accomplish the seller's main goals of reducing time on the market and maximizing profit.

The P that is often the most talked about when it comes to properties is price. Price is what people talk about to their friends and family, and one of the main criteria buyers consider when searching for a home. Deciding the right price takes market research and experience through not only the real estate market but the behavior of the target buyer.

The first item you will want to discuss with your agent is comparable properties in the area, so you will understand your competition and make sure that you measure up accordingly. Closed properties have the highest weight when it comes to appraisals, and it shows what people would actually pay for a similar property. You also want to look at the active and pending properties as well. I have had so many clients say to me "The neighbor's house is the same model as mine and is priced at $xxx,xxx and my house is better than theirs so we should list higher". This logic is flawed. Your house may be much better than the neighbors, but if they have it listed too high and it is just sitting on the market, then pricing it above theirs may result in your home doing the same. Don't just consider what other properties sold for, but also what they were listed at. The pending listings are a good way to check these, but since these are just pending prices, you don't know what offers were accepted. You see the list prices at the times offers were accepted and it stays this way until the sales are closed. Only then do you find out closing prices.

Looking at pricing the way an appraiser would is a good idea. An appraiser utilizes comparable sales and makes adjustments to allow for how your property matches up to the comparables. For instance if a recently sold comparable has three bathrooms and your similar property only has two bathrooms then the appraiser would adjust the price of your property's estimated worth based on this factor. Keep in mind that adjustments are never dollar for dollar. As an example, if you spend $30k renovating your kitchen you aren't going to sell your house for $30k more than the neighbor's house if the only difference is the condition of the kitchen.

Appraisers look at similar houses in the neighborhood with and without certain features to come up with a value. For example, if house 1 does not have a pool and sells for $130k, and identical house 2 has a pool and sells for $145k, then it is likely that the appraiser has placed a value of $15k on a pool in that neighborhood. Each neighborhood is different. There could be a neighborhood 5 miles with values on swimming pools set at $30k. This is why it is important to make sure that the agent you are working with is actually regularly working in your area, not just pulling up comparable sales and picking a random price.

Sometimes people set the price on their home because they think "This is what I want to make on my house, I'm just going to sit and wait until I make that." That mentality is detrimental to somebody that would actually like to sell their home.

Just because that is what you think your home is worth doesn't mean that the rest of the market will agree. Not being willing to move your price to accommodate the market will leave your home sitting for longer than others on the market resulting in a negative stigma.

Think of it like you're buying a car. You go to the car lot and there are 3 brand new cars of the same make and model, 2 of them are priced at $25,000 and the third is priced at $30,000. Every time a $25,000 car is sold it is replaced with another $25,000 car that is also the same. How long do you think that $30,000 will sit on the car lot? Probably a really long time and eventually people will start to ask "why has that car been on the lot so long?" Then even if there isn't a single thing wrong with it people will start to think "nobody else has wanted it, obviously there is something wrong with it." This is why it is important to drop your price if you aren't getting the level of action that is customary for your market and the rest of your marketing mix is correctly in line.

Your real estate agent can get statistics on your neighborhood and your entire market, and goals on traffic (showings of your home) should be set in advance. If, for some reason, you aren't reaching your goals you should change something in your marketing mix to increase traffic. Many times price is an easy way to do that. However, price doesn't just include the list price of your home. It also includes the ways that your home can be financed, the commission you are paying to the agent that brings a buyer to your home, and any closing costs you may be paying on behalf of the buyer. I have seen houses with lots of showings but no offers, then the seller adds a bonus to the buyer's agent, and there is an offer in a week. While agents aren't supposed to be biased on properties based on what they are being paid, I have seen many agents push a little harder to point out the benefits of a property that has a $1,500 bonus offered to them over the same home with no bonus. Offering to pay some of the buyers closing costs, paying for a home warranty, or perhaps giving an allowance for paint or flooring can all have a similar results.

When you make a change to your price, you want to monitor the way the market is viewing that change. There are a variety of metrics available to agents that allow them to see how many people are viewing your property and what action they are taking. You should be able to request custom reports from your agent and they will tell you exactly how many people are seeing your house online and if they are inquiring about it, sharing it with friends, looking at several photos, etc. If you are getting 1,000 views per week and only two showings, there is probably a problem with the way your home is displayed online or your price. In order to stay on top of your pricing and make sure your home is competitive it is best to have a conversation with your agent every 2 – 4 weeks to go over the different metrics they can provide for you and talk about strategy for the rest of your marketing campaign.

FIVE

Don't Buy A House Without Your Agent

By Sandy Casella

Can you find your next property by yourself? Absolutely. Should you? The answer to that depends entirely on how much you value your hard earned money and time.

Picture this, you and your spouse have decided you have been renting long enough, and perhaps it's time to buy your own place. Sunday afternoon you figure you will drive through one of the neighborhoods you like and you see an open house. You go into the open house and you both fall in love with the house and decide to buy it. Lucky for you, there happens to be a real estate agent there who offers to help you put an offer on the house. You meet the real estate agent at their office afterwards, sign the offer and to your good fortune the sellers accept it! Congratulations!

It is four months later and now that you have lived in the house for two months, reality is starting to set in. You went to register your little girl for school, and you realize that you are two streets over from the school district you wanted to be in, and now little Sally can't go to your school of choice. In talking to the neighbors, you find out that rumor has it that the previous owners were in deep financial difficulty and, as a result, were getting divorced. They had to sell the house; they had no choice. Your neighbor tells you that you probably could have purchased the house for significantly less. Your neighbor is so happy you moved in because the previous owners never took care of their home; they never saw them doing any maintenance to the house until it was time to sell. Now you start to realize that what you thought was a great deal may not have been. You begin to wonder if you made a mistake buying the house or wonder if you could have bought it for a much lower price.

Now imagine this scenario: you and your spouse decide to buy a home and you contact a real estate agent that you have heard good things about and that seems to have a good working knowledge of the area where you want to live. She/he invites you to their office to discuss your needs. You go over exactly what you are looking for in a home including what is important to you in terms of its location. You talk about the school you want your children to attend, how you get to work and what is the easiest and fastest way for you to get there. You share where you like to shop and the places you and your family find yourselves when you are enjoying family time.

Ask yourself what you are looking for in a home How many bedrooms do you need, where do you spend most of your time in the home? Is it in the kitchen, or perhaps watching sports in the family room? Do you want a big backyard or a smaller backyard with less maintenance? What other things do you absolutely have to have in your perfect home? Do you want the opportunity to renovate the home to your liking or do you want to simply move in and enjoy?

How much money can you comfortably afford to put towards a monthly mortgage payment? Do you have a pre-approval from the lender based on your income and credit worthiness? All of these things will determine what you can buy and what terms you can get from your lender. A good real estate agent can help you with all of this. A good deal with your lender can result in you saving thousands of dollars over the life of your mortgage which means more money in your pocket.

Now how will you find that perfect house? There are many methods your realtor can employ to help find your dream home, and it just may or may not be a home that is currently on the market. It could be one that was on the market and then was taken off for any number of reasons. It may be for sale by the owner, or it may be one that your realtor has knowledge through his or her marketing that the owner would like to sell it.

Once you find the home you want you again meet with your realtor, and you discuss what similar homes have sold for on the street and in the neighborhood. In conversation, you also discuss the condition of this home and what would be a fair offer price. Your agent then types up an offer for the home and then goes to work negotiating on your behalf to get you the right market substantiated price.

Fast forward four months and you have been in the house for two months. You meet up with the neighbors and you have a wonderful conversation about the neighborhood. You find out the previous owners are going to be missed by all of the neighbors as they were conscientious about their investment. You decide you bought the perfect house and you couldn't be happier.

As in any profession, the very best people in the real estate field will be drawn toward higher paying full-service business models while those with the least experience and expertise will be drawn to models built around low cost.

SIX

The Power of Multiple Listing Service (MLS)

By John Gluch

The information age has brought with it an unprecedented rate of growth in all forms of information and technology. The advent of technologies such as the internet and smart phones has completely revolutionized the way people search for (and sell) homes. According to a joint study by Google and The National Association of Realtors, more than 90% of people begin their home searches online. Thus the internet has changed the way that buyers shop and agents market properties. This chapter will focus on the various ways in which to market your home for sale online.

In August of 2014, the real estate marketing monster Zillow.com purchased Trulia.com to create the largest online home sales platform in existence. While each website continues to operate separately, the purchase spurred months of conversations on what the future of home sales might look like. As a real estate professional of more than a dozen years and a millennial (I barely make the cut as I was born in 1980) who has spent much of his adult life online I too have followed this trend with great interest.

To begin, let us follow the order of events that gets most homes posted on sites like Zillow. For the purpose of this conversation, I'll limit my comments to Zillow since it is the most popular real estate website online. The typical order of events begins with a home seller contacting a real estate agent who then lists their home on the Multiple Listing System (MLS) in that area. These systems are controlled by the local board of Realtors and may only be utilized by licensed real estate agents who are members of the board. Once posted on the MLS, the home is then marketed to other Realtors in that area who may have buyers looking for a home similar to the one just listed. Before the internet came along this is where it all ended as local real estate agents were the only ones with full access to information on all of the homes listed for sale in the area and buyers would meet with agents to learn about what homes might be for sale that fit their specific needs. Listings used to come out via a monthly MLS book and hot sheets were used for disseminating information such as price changes, etc.

Enter the internet. Now, those listings are syndicated by local real estate brokerages and given out to companies like Zillow to publish on their website. There is a small delay in this process, and not all of the information related to the listing is provided to Zillow but the main features and benefits of the home along with pictures are all shared openly. It's important to note that Zillow is designed to be a consumer-facing site. It is easy and fun to look at and shows people what they are interested in seeing. The MLS, on the other hand, is designed to be agent facing and is designed with the professional Realtor in mind. Its power is far greater on the agent side, and there are innumerable ways for agents to use the MLS to research homes in ways Zillow just cannot match. Once a home listing makes it to Zillow, it is there for the whole world to see, thus broadening the reach of the listing. While Zillow and other sites like it are wonderful resources for home buyers, sellers, and those who just enjoy looking at houses, all of the information disseminated on it must be taken with a grain of salt and a realtor should be consulted for further details.

As I said above, this is how most homes make it on Zillow. People wanting to market their home as For Sale By Owner (FSBO) can easily post their own home on Zillow for no charge and forgo the hiring of a real estate agent. This begs the question, does a home seller need to hire an agent to sell their home or is putting it on Zillow themselves just as good? For now, we will put aside the many benefits that come with having the assistance of someone who has made it his or her full-time profession to sell homes and just look at the marketing side of things. I recently had the opportunity to perform about as pure a test as can be performed measuring the marketing power of Zillow.

In January of 2014, my wife and I decided to sell our home in Scottsdale, Arizona. As an experiment, I first listed my home on Zillow and tested the listing for two weeks before putting it on our area MLS. I hired a professional photographer on our team that I use for all of our listings and had him photograph the home. I then posted it on Zillow and syndicated it to every other major real estate website. I live in a high demand area, and we had recently remodeled the home in a style that is very popular right now. Over the course of the two weeks that I had the home on

Zillow I had a total of four calls… no showings and no offers. After two weeks, I listed the home on the MLS with the exact same pictures, price and descriptions as I used on Zillow. Within one week I had 13 showings and four offers, two of which were for over my asking price. I ended up signing an offer for $12,000 over my asking price, and we closed three weeks later.

This simple little experiment is a dramatic example of the marketing power of a system like your local MLS and more importantly the real estate agents that subscribe to it. To help understand why there is such a huge difference in the results obtained we must start from a basic understanding of where Zillow makes its money and where Realtor's make theirs. Zillow is 100% free to the consumer, and its only revenue stream is from advertisers, the lion's share of whom are realtors. For a fee, real estate agents can advertise their services on Zillow with the hope that consumers will contact them when they are ready to buy or sell a home. Zillow has no incentive to help get your home sold. All they care about it generating website traffic and getting that traffic pointed in the direction of one of their paying customers, i.e. a realtor. On the other hand, agents only make money when they actually sell homes. Zillow wants advertisers, and realtors want people's homes sold. The incentives are entirely different as are the results.

This system is based on the fundamental idea that people do not want to make what is likely to be the biggest financial decision of their lives without the help of a professional. This idea has proven to be true time and time again. As the internet began to grow in reach, several "flat fee" brokerages including companies like Redfin sprung up. These companies are discount brokerages with very limited services that base their business models on the idea that consumers would rather save money than have a full-service real estate agent. Time has shown that consumers get what they pay for, and most of these companies have either gone out of business or are still putting along with little steam left. The model itself was broken. As in any profession, the very best people in the real estate field will be drawn toward higher paying full-service business models while those with the least experience and expertise will be drawn to models built around low cost.

The very best agents have embraced these new marketing platforms and do an amazing job highlighting their client's homes on the web. In the information age, people want to do some basic research on their own, especially in the beginning of their search and then when they get serious they want the trusted expertise of someone who sells houses day in and day out. This has even become true of the agents themselves. For instance, if you Google my name you will see me on dozens of websites and find 100's of reviews from my past clients. Consumers now can not only research the home they are interested in buying, but the agent they will use to do so. In the end, this availability of information is highly valuable to consumers and will serve to produce better agents to serve them.

Now let's quickly go back to the example of my selling my own home. Let's say I had gotten a great offer for my home from a buyer who found it on Zillow or even from a friend who knew I was selling and made me an offer. Would I have sold? No. I personally just could not have slept without knowing what I could have gotten by listing the home on the MLS. In this case even a full price offer would have netted me $12k less than I ended up with. There just simply is no substitute for the marketing power of a local full-service agent using the local MLS. It turns out you really do get what you pay for!

SEVEN

Leverage The Power Of Social Media

By Jonathan Lahey

According to the Merriam Webster Dictionary, social media is described as "forms of electronic communication (as websites for social networking and micro blogging) through which users create online communities to share information, ideas, personal messages, and other content (such as videos).

Social media websites where you can easily have a presence include Facebook, Twitter, LinkedIn, Google+, Instagram, Pinterest, Reddit, YouTube, Foursquare, Flickr, Photobucket, Picasa, and many more. There is no cost for you to create a profile on these websites although some, like LinkedIn, do offer a premium membership level at a minimum cost per month.

Let's rewind back to the early 2000's, back when my real estate career was just getting underway. The concept of "Social Media" marketing back then meant marketing to your social circles either by "Word of Mouth" advertising or passing out flyers to your circle of friends. In the early 2000's, Facebook was not the media giant it is today. Instagram and Pinterest did not even exist and Google+ was just an idea. To spread your message across thousands, or potentially hundreds of thousands of your peers cost a lot of money. Back then, your typical real estate agent depended on direct mail or printed ads to expose the homes they were selling to the mass public. If you claimed to have social media presence in the early 2000's, it usually meant you had a "Friendster" account with testimonials from your sphere of influence, or you had some type of blog, either powered by Xanga or Blogger (blogspot.com).

Fast forward to today. Your "web-savvy" real estate agents know the power of social media, and they take full advantage of social media on a daily basis. Even the least savvy of real estate agents has a personal Facebook profile while most utilize the "Business" profile as well. My real estate team and I personally use Facebook to not only connect with our clients, but to also spread our brand, and to expose our inventory of homes to the world. Rather than depending on direct mail to get my marketing message spread around to my target audience, I use social media to get my message across to the masses quickly and effectively. I can post a photo of a house on Facebook, for example, and along with a catchy line that speaks directly to my buyers. That photo will be seen by my network of friends, and my friends' network of friends as well. The more people "like" your Facebook photos/posts, the more networks of friends you can infiltrate. You never know if one of your friends in your network is looking to purchase a home in your neighborhood. Better yet, you don't know if they are looking for a home just like yours!

As a team, we generate hundreds of home buyers each year through social media marketing, and each year many of the home buyers we generate through our proven marketing system ends up buying a home with us. My real estate team is social proof that social media marketing works! Did I mention that social media is FREE? You can get your message spread out to the mass really fast at no cost.

Now, what if you have a very small network of friends? What if you can't get your friends to comment, or "like" your posts? What if you don't have the time to wait for your Facebook post to go viral? Well, here's the secret to how I get my Facebook posts on top of everyone's newsfeed. Simple, I pay for it! I have found that Facebook Ads are a great way to spread your message to a very targeted audience. As an example, for a mere $25 I am able to expose my newest "home for sale" ad to a super-targeted audience of over 7,000 people. Facebook allows me to target my audience by age, occupation, location, interest, spending habits, home ownership, education level, etc. Compare this to direct mail. Your typical direct mail postcard postage alone will cost $0.34 per piece (in 2014). If I send out 7,000 postcards, the postage alone will cost me $2,380, and that's not considering the cost to print out the postcards, or to buy a targeted mailing list.

How much you should expect to spend on Facebook is up to you. Technically, you don't have to spend anything. You can just depend on your friends to spread your post around by liking it, or commenting on your post - today's version of word-of-mouth advertising. But if you do decide to invest in advertising, Facebook can help you decide how much to spend. Facebook is good at predicting how much exposure your budget will most likely get you.

To create an ad on Facebook, you need:

- **A Facebook account.** I will not explain to you how to create an account here; I'm sure there are lots of tutorials out there for you to review and follow.

- **A message or an offer for your audience.** It could be an "Open House" you're trying to promote. It could be a "Just Reduced" message you're trying to spread. It could also be a "Just Listed" blast to your friends. Whatever you're trying to share, that's your message. In order to make your message stand out, make sure your message speaks to (and about) your audience directly!

- **An attention grabbing photo.** If your ad is to sell your house, the best photo is either the front of the house, the kitchen or the family room.

- **A defined audience.** I know it sounds silly, but it's really important that you know who you are trying to reach. In regards to the house you are selling, is it ideal for a first-time home buyer, or is it ideal for a move-up buyer?

I'm going to give you a real life example with my real estate team. We have been running an agent recruiting campaign ad on Facebook for the past year. Our goal is to double the size of our team within the year.

Our ad offers a guaranteed $60k income to real estate agents. The offer is attractive to real estate agents because we also specified that they do not have to do any prospecting or cold calls to earn our $60k income guarantee. Sounds attractive right? Here is the problem: We did not specify who we wanted to attract. We did not identify who would be an ideal team member. When we ran that ad, we had no idea if we wanted brand new agents, or if we wanted experienced agents? Did we want people who are just thinking of getting their real estate license, or did we want people who are at the end of their real estate career?

Because we did not target properly, we got applications from many unqualified people. Learn from our mistake. Don't waste your ad budget on exposing your message to an audience that is not ideal for your ad.

- **A landing page.** A landing page is a web page or website your audience arrives at after clicking on your ad. This page needs to look and sound the same as your ad. Use the same color scheme and theme. Use the same font. This page should reiterate your message on the Facebook ad. The purpose of the landing page is to capture your audience's contact information. The landing page simply captures your audience's contact info (or at the very least, name and email) so that you can effectively follow up with these people (whether to sell them a product like a house or to follow up and make sure all of their questions have been answered).

- **A call to action.** A call to action tells your audience what to do to obtain the information you are offering. Some of our best call to actions include statements like "Call Jonathan at ###-##### for a no obligation consultation" or "Go to www.TopNewListings.com to get the most up-to-date list of homes for sale in your area!" Be specific and concise in your call to action messaging.

- **Performance tracking.** Go to the Facebook Ad Manager, and you will find the results of your ad campaign. You can see how much it cost you to generate one click or one post engagement. The better your message speaks to your audience; you will find the cost will be lower. Facebook will also tell you how many people clicked on your ad.

Your landing page should tell you how many people fill out a request form to obtain the information you are offering. You want to pay attention to what percentage of people who landed on your landing page actually fill out the form.

With these 7 things in your back pocket, you will be able to leverage Social Media to help you spread your marketing message across to your targeted audience quickly, and effectively.

EIGHT

Creating Value From The Inside Out

By Rudy L. Kusuma

Selling your home is probably one of the most important tasks you will encounter in your life. It took you a while before you decided to purchase it, and now it's time to sell your largest asset, so of course you expect to get top dollar for it.

According to the National Association of Realtors, nearly two-thirds of the people surveyed who sold their own homes on their own say they wouldn't do it again themselves. Primary reasons included setting a price, marketing handicaps, liability concerns, and time constraints. When deciding upon a realtor, consider two or three. Be as wary of quotes that are too low as those that are too high.

All realtors are not the same! A professional realtor knows the market and has information on past sales, current listings, a marketing plan, and will provide their background and references. Evaluate each candidate carefully on the basis of their experience, qualifications, enthusiasm and personality. Be sure you choose someone you trust and feel confidence they will do a good job on your behalf.

If you choose to sell on your own, you can still talk to a realtor. Many are more than willing to help do-it-your-selfers with paperwork, contracts, etc. and should problems arise, you now have someone you can readily call upon for assistance.

Appearances Do Matter – Make them Count!

Appearance is so critical when selling your home. The look and feel of your home will generate a greater emotional response than any other factor. Prospective buyers react to what they see, hear, feel, and smell even though you may have priced your home to sell.

Instead of installing boring and traditional 'for sale' signs, use one that is catchy, big, long, and colorful – create a WOW factor! Buyers are more likely to stop by or at least recall "that house with the big FOR SALE sign". It is very common for potential buyers to stop in the middle of the road and obtain the information about a property.

You may also want to put a "Talking House®" sign in front of your home. Talking House® is a radio transmitter with a recorded message with information about your home. Imagine how quickly your home would sell if your agent were there 24 hours a day, 7 days a week standing at the curb talking with every prospective buyer that stopped by. That's what it's like with Talking House! Your home sells itself to every prospective buyer that drives by. Prospects stop, and "tune in" on their car radio. They hear all of the features that make your home special.
Your home stands out in a crowded marketplace, so it sells faster for top dollar! According to the Newspaper Association of America, the #1 source of information for home buyers comes from driving around! If your home isn't talking, no one is listening.

Get it Spic n' Span Clean and Fix Everything Even If it Seems Insignificant

Scrub, scour, tidy up, straighten, get rid of the clutter, declare war on dust, repair squeaks, fix the light switch that doesn't work, and the tiny crack in the bathroom mirror because these can be deal-killers, and you'll never know what turns buyers off. Remember, you're not just competing with other resale homes, but brand-new ones as well.

Allow Prospective Buyers to Visualize Themselves in Your Home

The last thing you want prospective buyers to feel when viewing your home is they may be intruding into someone's life. Avoid clutter such as too many knick-knacks, piles of personal mail, untidy closets, etc. Decorate in neutral colors, such as white or beige and place a few carefully chosen items to add warmth and character around the home. You can enhance the attractiveness of your home with a well-placed vase of flowers or potpourri in the bathroom. Home-decor magazines are great for innovative design tips.

Selling Your Home For Top Dollar

Interior Designers, Home Staging, and Custom Brand New Furniture

A professional interior designer and crew can stage your home with brand new custom furniture, organize , and take care of other aspects such as lighting, flow and function, color combinations, patterns, and other things you and I might not even notice like smell and temperature. Below are some great before and after photos, each image shows a dramatic difference between un-staged and staged.

Before showing your home to potential buyers, make sure your home is ready. The simple four Cs to determine whether or not your home is ready are:

- **Clean.** Everything has to be clean and spotless. This will make your home look like a new model home.

- **Clutter-free.** Make everything neat and tidy so the potential buyers can see the space the house has to offer instead of one's personal belongings.

- **Color.** Neutral colors will help potential buyers imagine themselves living there with their own furniture.

- **Creativity.** All of these things should leave a couple of good impressions in buyers minds to remember the home by after they finish looking at dozens of other homes.

Deal Killer Odors Must Go!

You may not realize it, but odd smells like traces of food, pets and smoking odors can kill deals quickly. If prospective buyers know you have a dog, or that you smoke, they'll start being aware of odors and seeing stains that may not even exist. Don't leave any clues.

The Goal is to have Multiple Offers

When you maximize your home's marketability, you will most likely attract more than one prospective buyer. It is much better to have several buyers because they will compete with each other; a single buyer will end up competing with you.

NINE

Staging To Sell

By Ahmad Shalforoshzadeh

Pre-packing and de-cluttering take on a big part of home selling preparedness. Your house needs to be neat, clean and orderly in order to appeal to the majority of buyers in the market today.

Things to think about:

- Does your house feel spacious?

- Is your house clean from top to bottom?

- How does your garage look?

- If one area of your house is unfinished and you use it for storage, what does it looks like?

- Pre-pack all items you do not need while your house is for sale

- Decide on a place for storage

Curb Appeal (Front, Back and Side Yard)

Having an attractive exterior will create a lasting impression. When a buyer passes by your home, they will be eager to stop and view the interior if your home is maintained both inside and outside and appears well-cared for.

Things to think about:

- Make a list of what needs to be done.

- What major and minor repairs are needed?

- Sweep or shovel walkways, driveways, patio/deck (salt in the winter).

- Put up some flowers or winter arrangements on your front porch.

- Maintain a nice and clean front, back and side yard.

Depersonalizing

Depersonalization is an important step for selling your home. This can be a tough process, but emotionally you need to let go. Once you have made your decision to sell the house, and it's time to move you need to remove your identity from the house. Disconnecting yourself from your house will allow potential buyers to emotionally connect with living there instead of feeling like guests.

Things to think about:

- Store away all personal and family photos.

- Remove all memorabilia.

- Pre-pack books, children's toys, and games that do not appeal to a wide range of buyers.

- Do you have belongings that could potentially turn off buyers like mounted animal trophies? If so, consider putting them in storage.

Flooring

Flooring is another important part of home sale preparedness. Buyers want a home that is move in ready. One of the top selling features buyers look for when purchasing a home is up-to-date flooring.

Things to think about:

- What is the condition of your carpet?

- What color is the carpet?

- What style is your carpet? Cut pile or Berber?

- If you need to replace your carpet, do you need to re-do every room? If not select something that will work with the rest of the carpeting in the house.

- What style of vinyl flooring do you have?

- Does it need to be replaced?

- Do you have hardwood?

- Does it need to be refinished?

- Do you have hardwood under your carpet?

Furniture Placement and Lighting

Proper furniture placement will display a room to its full potential. Keep in mind buyers will walk through each room, If you have excessive furniture that clutters and makes a room seem small then you should consider putting it in storage while your home is on the market. Lighting is also a key factor for making a good impression. Make sure to have all lights on for pictures and showings. When your furniture and lighting are properly placed, they will allow buyers to see the function of each room and prime features.

Things to think about:

- How much furniture is in each room?

- How is your furniture placed?

- What size is your furniture?

- What is the condition of your furniture?

- Do you need to rent or purchase new furniture?

- How much lighting do you have in each room?

- What is the condition of permanent light fixtures?

Home Inspection

Have your home inspected before it is listed. An inspection will determine if there are any major repairs needed and they can be addressed before the house goes on the market. This will also show the buyer and their agent that you have been proactive. When it comes to finding the right home inspector, a real estate agent is your best source for recommending someone. Once the inspection is completed, you will be able to decide what the next steps are in preparing your home for sale.

Things to think about:

- How old is your house?

- What is the condition of your foundation?

- Do your lights flicker or are any breakers or fuses blown?

- Do you have aluminum wiring or knob and tube?

- What is the condition of your plumbing?

- Are your windows in good condition?

- Do you have any water problems?

- Have you had problems with mold and mildew?

- How old is your furnace?

- Is your roof in good condition?

Main Selling Rooms

The overall impression of your entire home is essential. You need to make sure that rooms create extraordinary first impressions, Buyers will focus on your main selling rooms which include the front entrance, kitchen and living area.

Things to think about:

Front Entrance

- How do the rooms look from where you are standing?
- Does your entrance feel spacious?

Kitchen

- How does the kitchen look and feel when you walk into it?
- Identify which areas require changes
- How does your pantry look?

Living Room

- Does this room feel warm and inviting?
- How is your furniture arranged?
- Are there any repairs upgrades that need to be done?

Dining Room

Does this room show its function?

How is the furniture arranged?

Family Room

- What is the focal point in this room?

- Are there any repairs or upgrades that need to be done?

- How is the furniture positioned?

Master Bedroom

- Do you feel calm walking into this room?

- How is your furniture positioned?

- Are there any repairs or upgrade that needs to be done?

Air Quality/Odor/Pets/Holidays

Most people overlook these, but they important parts of home selling preparedness as well. Buyers want to envision themselves living in the house. A powerful odor can deter them from wanting to see the house. Pets with dirty litter boxes or uncleaned yard space with animal waste can be a deal killers. Not everyone loves pets and some have allergies which could be a concern if they are potentially interested in purchasing your home.

Things to think about:

- What year was your house built?

- What time of year are you selling?

- Are there going to be any holidays during that time?

- Have you had any water issues?

- Check for mold or mildew

- Inspect your smoke and carbon monoxide detectors and replace if needed
- Avoid cooking with strong seasonings and foods that have lingering aromas
- Remove your pets while the house is on the market
- Remove any signs of the pets e.g. food and water bowls, toys, litter box, leashes
- If your pets must stay in the house, hide them during showings
- Keep litter boxes clean and out of sight

Paint

If your house is painted in very bright or unusual colors, potential buyers may be turned off or worse yet, feel that they can negotiate down your asking price. Neutral colors are warm to the eye and most buyers want to live in a house for a while before deciding if they want to change the paint color.

Things to think about:

- When was the last time you painted your house?
- Do you have a warm color palette in your house?
- Do your walls need to be painted a neutral color?
- If they are already neutral, do they need a fresh coat of paint?
- Do you have wallpaper?
- Do your doors and trim need a fresh coat of paint?
- Put a fresh coat of paint on the ceiling to give the entire room a clean look

Updates and Repairs

Having an objective outlook toward your house will determine what updates and repairs are necessary. Based on your timeline and budget you should be able to identify things to be done to improve the overall presentation of your home. Buyers today are willing to pay more for a house that has been well maintained, so show them your home is in turn-key condition.

Things to think about:

- What is your timeline and budget?

- What updates have you been putting off?

- What repairs are needed?

- What is the condition of your windows?

- What is the condition of your permanent light fixtures?

- What are the conditions of your doors and trim?

- Do you have any holes or cracks in your walls?

TEN

The Investment and Second Home Seller

By Jared W. Jones

If you are an investor or corporate owner, this section of the book will hopefully add immense value to your understanding and give you some very good insights on potential problems that can arise if you do not take certain precautions.

Who will get the most from this section? If you buy mortgage notes, and will likely process through a foreclosure to then liquidate the home, this section is for you. If you want to flip real estate and do short term holds, you will undoubtedly be in precarious positions that one must encounter and work through when the "deal" has proverbial "hair" on it. Maybe you are an acquisition manager for a large entity or corporate buyer. The following is very good information to help you understand in just a few pages, the pitfalls and surprises you can encounter and how to manage them.

Is the Home Insured Properly?

Corporate and out of area owners are the most common buyer types to own a home all cash. Depending on the transaction, the insurance policy can completely fall through the cracks. Imagine you buy a home, and gosh forbid, the home turns into a swimming pool or bonfire, and then you find out that you don't have the proper coverage. Not much needs to be said about this. But even if you have coverage, make sure it isn't so full of loopholes you are virtually left in the cold if something were to happen to your home especially since the home is likely part or full-time vacant.

Home Owner Associations (HOAs)

Depending on the area of the country in which you reside, an HOA may be known by different titles but its most likely there for the same reason. HOAs are formed in all neighborhoods across the country to help maintain continuity and the standards for each area. However, left unchecked, HOAs can cause absolute havoc in the selling process for investors and corporate owners.

First off, corporate owners can buy a home without a completely clean title, and it can include delinquent HOA fees. Foreclosure sales are the most common place for this. You can end up having months of delinquent dues and thousands in collection fees for which you are responsible. If you do not pay these in a timely manner after taking possession, an HOA can commence foreclosure! In Nevada, where I sell real estate, there are laws debating whether or not the lien holder (owner) who is wiped off of the title has any right of recourse to reclaim their home. Buying foreclosures through "HOA sales" has become quite a big business. Auction buyers who pay a few thousand dollars can actually now be legitimate owners of HOA liens. At the time of my writing, this is practice is up for debate.

You do not want to let HOA fees on your home to get out of hand. Also, do not trust the collection companies and HOA management firms at face value with what their statements may claim you owe. If you do find yourself in a position where you acquire a home you need to sell that has extensive past HOA liens, call the local Real Estate Division's Ombudsman's office, and they will tell you if the HOA you are working with is on the right side of what the law says. I have seen one of my clients receive invoices from HOA Collection companies for oil stains in the driveway of a home purchased at Foreclosure Auction in excess of $5,000! The home was valued in the $100 to $200,000 range and had a total of over $14,000 in expected penalties and late fees. We negotiated down 70% and, needless to say; the HOA and the collection company were eventually involved in a class action lawsuit.

Often, corporate owners underestimate their property needs after tenants who provide upkeep move out and a few weeks after the home is vacated and on market, fines and violations start rolling in. This can complicate closing on your home due to unforeseen expenses showing up on your closing statement, and it is completely avoidable. The stricter the HOA in your area, the more maintenance on the exterior your home will require. Consider that in planning for the sale.

Evictions and CFKs: Unwanted Guests

Sometimes, investors purchase homes with unplanned guests. I managed a partnership this year; that got a great deal, but had a house full of people who were living in the home unlawfully.

In this case – you have two options. One is amicable and friendly, the other is more intrusive to the occupant, and BOTH have a place in removing unwanted (unplanned may be more kind) guests. In my career, with a high volume of personal investment experience as well as dealing with corporate owners, I've dealt with more than 500 of these types of events, possibly as many as a 1,000. The best thing to do is communicate. This is typically done by posting the home and advising the occupant(s) of your contact information as owner, and the fact you have options for them to (preferably) transition amicably to a new living space.

A 'Cash for Keys' agreement (CFK) is an upfront agreement signed by the owner or their representative, and the occupant. This agreement lays out the timelines for the occupant to move out of the home and on presumed "good behavior." The ideal goal of a successful CFK is the occupant(s) leaves the home in broom swept condition, free of personal property, and with all fixtures intact. This is very valuable for a corporate owner because it insulates you from having to perform personal property evictions if excessive valuables are left behind. Obviously it also more likely leaves the home in good condition, making transition to the market for sale much easier. A typical payout to execute and move out of an occupant under a CFK agreement can be as little as $500 or as much as $7,000. The value of the payouts typically hinge on the value of the asset and the length of time an occupant is given to prepare to move out.

Eviction is typically used when all other processes fail. I highly recommend you use and consult a good local attorney who deals with evictions as their mainstream of business.

Important If you are buying a home with the intent to put it back on the market, and the home is occupied by an unplanned occupant - meaning you don't know how the transition will go when you purchase it– be very mindful of the local eviction timelines. This is absolutely critical because in some states, evictions can be executed swiftly in weeks, and some can take several months. Either way, an eviction can add significantly to your holding cost prior to sale.

Utilities and Recurring Services

I have seen investors try to save money by leaving utilities off/down in their homes. This can cause death of the plant life, and cause HOA violations rather quickly. Secondly it can delay the maid services and contractors from preparing the home for sale.

At minimum, power and water but you must be careful to consider heating and cooling fuel. Through summers in Las Vegas, a home's market appeal is impacted negatively if it's ambient interior temperature is higher than 80 degrees. In the winter, it's highly recommended to leave the heat setting at 68 degrees to keep the home warm enough that pipes don't freeze. I have seen homes that suffered massive damages when pipes in their ceilings burst, caved in the upper wallboards, and caused serious mold problems.

If you are in moderate to very cold climates in winter, you should consider winterizing a vacant home. This means that a company will come in and vacuum out the lines and shut down all plumbing. It's the safest thing to do when temperatures in the area stay around or below freezing for extended periods. When you purchase a home, you should de-winterize for the home inspection. However, if this occurs in the dead of winter, you should plan to winterize again following the inspection. This may be a cost you want to include for the buyer when negotiating your contract.

Important If you have potential electrical hazards, make sure you do not turn on the power unless the master breaker is off, or consider leaving it off altogether until an electrical contractor has reviewed and remedied any open wiring. Another common mishap I see when investors takeover new homes is the laundry hook-up flooding. The previous owner moves their appliances out and leaves the water line that fed their washing machine wide open. The water company opens the water and the home floods in the area around it. Same goes for ice maker lines that are connected to the refrigerator/freezer. If you can, shut down the master water line before turning on the water in a home that was recently vacated that you now want to sell.

Condition Concerns – To Repair or Not To Repair?

When flipping a home back to the marketplace, deciding to repair will hinge on three key areas:

1. Market Conditions at the Time of Sale

2. Type of Highest Paying Buyer

3. Tendency for Vandalism

Market conditions at the time of sale. When considering whether to repair or not, the market conditions will come into play. To drive the most money to the bottom line, you must consider if the market is seller favored and homes sell quickly or if it's a buyer's market and homes will take a little longer to have a successful sale. When it's a quick market, you typically will not get a great margin more for the trouble and expense of repairs. In a hot market, homes are bid to the very top of the market with conditions not affecting sales like they do in a slower market. On the other hand, in a slow market, you want every advantage to attract the few buyers in the market place to your home.

Type of likely highest paying buyer. This is a big deal with the modern world of lending being so strict on a "Property qualifying" for the loan. If your likely buyer is FHA or VA, they will order an appraisal of the home, and they will take into consideration safety concerns, and various maintenance issues. These can come up and cause delays if not addressed in advance. This doesn't mean that you have to have a sparkling clean floor to ceiling rehab on a home just to fly with these two loan types, but it does mean that aged roofs, stucco cracks, a loose porch or patio cover, and other items that have just eroded over time could be flagged on a report and repairs be conditioned to be completed or the buyer's loan cannot be funded.

Tendency for Vandalism. This is a practical consideration for repairs. If the home is a target for a weekend party by local teenagers or likely to be "repainted" with spray paint as it sits vacant waiting to sell, then repairs in these circumstances may just not make good sense.

Dealing with Data and When to Sell

This is key. I picked this topic out for this particular section of this book because typically corporate sellers have the ability to choose when the time is right to sell. Often, they have tenants in their homes, so selling is more strategic and can be delayed if it makes sense to do so. I have purchased investment properties for myself across four different states. One thing I have noticed in every market place is there are cyclical seller's markets. If you can plan the exit on the sale of an asset in this way, pick the best time when homes are absorbed easily. As an example, Las Vegas is busiest from the end of February until the end of October. I have friends in Toronto who say that the summer is actually dead for them. Florida is busiest during the winter season when the snowbirds arrive. Bottom line is to check the data trends and ask a local professional to give you input ahead of the sale. Get good deals buying when you are out of the seller's market and then get those deals on the market when buyers are swooping in during the busy season. Why fight it, right!?

Dealing with a Dog

The Dog is the quintessential hard to sell home, and I have seen some doozies. There is the home that has the railroad tracks in the backyard. There is a half million dollar house that just so happens to be one of three in the entire subdivision that backs up to a four lane road. There is the condo where your tenant owned a cat whose spirit still resides there, or the oddball house that has some strange oddity like a front door around the side, a split level plan, or a rear neighbor who has a 12 foot grade looking right down into your home's rear yard eliminating any hope of privacy. In LasVegas, in the middle of the desert of all places, there is a pig farm and I have corporate owners who have never been to the home they own there in the area, and I am trying to describe for them the aromas that emit from around a housing of 300 swine 2 blocks away, and how to consider this odor when pricing their home.

First, don't ignore the Dog when pricing the home. Add on to the price for things that make your asset superior to the neighboring sales but don't ignore the fact that there is a freeway running behind your home when the neighbors had the good fortune of backing up to a park. Price it right otherwise buyers will walk in with those higher expectations that come with the price set, and be disappointed and run from the property before giving serious consideration. Don't under price it either. Just price it fairly.

Second, try and soften the concern in setup. If you live on a busy street, hopefully you have some way to dampen the noise. This can be a pool water feature or a wireless Jambox playing some jazz next to the patio set. If you are dealing with odors in the home, do not make the mistake of just changing out the flooring and not treating the area underneath. Contractors will take your orders to change the flooring and not treat underneath. This will not eliminate the odor in all likelihood, and you will be frustrated weeks later when buyers report back that they smell something.

Third, make sure to make the property look its best in photography. You can do a property a world of good through a great looking internet presence. The photos will get the traffic and the more traffic you can drive, the chances go up that the right buyer will see the home. A hard-to-sell home needs triple the traffic of a hindrance free home, so this part of the process is key. You can't misrepresent the home in photos, but you can position the challenges visibly in a way where you get more traffic than the neighboring home that doesn't have near the challenges. That is what great marketing is all about.

Proper Care for Vacant Homes

Make sure you hire an agent that is prepared to check on your home weekly when it's vacant. This is key. I have sold many, many homes for corporate owners, and empty homes can have epic problems, These can be minimized through frequent checking. When you file an insurance claim, and your agent has recent reports showing exactly when things went wrong, you will be glad you hired that agent, I assure you.

Vendors are our partners. Lawn maintenance and an occasional reoccurring maid service to keep the inside clean are critical to keeping the appeal high on a given property. These vendors are allies that keep an eye on the property and report any issues that arise. It's important to tell lawn and pool vendors who are frequently on premises to look around and call the broker promptly if they see any issues.

Looking Out For Code Issues

Code enforcement isn't too extreme in my market place, but it can be in others. In Las Vegas, you have to watch for out of control landscaping, debris in the yard, and pools that go from blue to green. These are the most common issues here locally, but they are relatively minor if you react quickly when they notified of their presence.

In many markets, if the home is old and falling over, there is a danger of massive fines and even demolition of the home! Ten years ago, I was at an investment and corporate owner liquidation conference, and there were stories circling of homes that would be there one day, and gone the next – completely demolished for runaway and ignored code violations! I couldn't believe it because that is so far removed from my marketplace. Treatment is pretty much the same: Be proactive. Call them, work together and manage the concern with them swiftly.

Mitigating Theft Hazards

Corporate sellers typically have a much higher concern of theft of the assets in their home because these properties are not owner occupied. Over the years I have seen every type of theft imaginable from pool pumps, major appliances, roof mounted AC units, and copper piping torn right out of the walls. I have had literally hundreds of assets that by the very nature of who owned them, made them a distinct target and had to learn many tricks to keep them safe. Here are just a few of those tips:

Padlock the garage doors and side gates. The garage door is a pipeline to remove the largest fixtures out of the home. Padlock it and unplug the garage door opener while it's vacant. Padlock side gates as well as these are exit #2.

Use as much signage as possible. Vacant homes are noticed first by nosy neighbors. This is the first time you will appreciate this, and as such they will watch out for your home and be QUICK to call you when things don't look right. Make sure they have your contact information readily at their disposal and post a for sale sign in front of the home as soon as you can.

Theft deterrent stickers. We put stickies on nicer appliances that look like Government issued warning labels that have a police badge on them and they state that each item is GPS tracked. We use these for pool equipment and major appliances. When we started using them, thefts went down immediately. I have to thank Eric Roth and Bryan Pelican locally with that stroke of brilliance.

Print name and number on large exterior equipment. Pool pumps and exterior housing theft will go down if you stencil your name or representative's name and their phone number on piece of equipment.

A/C Cages. Most marketplaces have vendors and contractors who will lease A/C cages to make sure they aren't stolen. Theft of AC units in Las Vegas have been very high. It's worth it to spend $200 to $300 on a cage to prevent a $5,000 HVAC unit from walking away.

Sealing. This is the ultimate in home protection! Sealing is literally turning a home into a tank! Every single door and window is literally boarded down or screwed down with sheet metal. I personally opt for the latter. These are leased and typically cost around $500 to $1,000 to have a custom seal setup put on a home. Typically sealing is used in the rehab portion of the selling process or for homes that will be marketed in as is condition and never rehabbed to sell.

In the end, it is the buyer's evaluation that matters. Buyers make their assessments by comparing your property with others that offer like features and are in a similar condition to yours.

ELEVEN

Buying and Selling Equestrian Estates

By Kirstin Kutchuk

Marketing and selling ranches and equestrian estates are an art and skill. Whether you are buying or selling in an equestrian community, it is imperative that you hire an agent who understands horse people and horse properties.

The character of an equestrian property is of special interest to me. There is quite a variety of Equestrian properties including ranches, equestrian estates, gentlemen farms, hobby farms, horse properties and land for sale. All of these require an agent that not only knows the area in which they work, but they need to have specialized knowledge of horses. Equestrian property can be difficult to buy; the following will help you through this process.

Buying: Don't Horse Around With the Details

Are you searching for an equine estate on the real estate market? Riding, raising and keeping horses is undeniably connected to our nation's oldest traditions and every region of the country presents an array of hobby farms, picture-perfect ranches, and equestrian properties.

Purchasing an equestrian property involves a lot more than simply finding enough land to keep a horse. There are trail access, property drainage, zoning restrictions and many more issues to address. An equestrian property specialist will know what to look for in a suitable equestrian property and keep on top of community and neighborhood trends regarding equestrian issues. Don't take chances when purchasing your dream ranch, consult a professional.

Real estate agents that specialize in properties where homeowners can also house their horses often must go the extra furlong to close the deal. They not only have to please potential buyers with the property's look and size, but they also must provide suitable stabling for horses.

Equestrian real estate brokers in Southern California report as much as a 50% increase in sales year to year from 2012 to 2013. Rising boarding fees in the United States and abroad are prompting owners to keep their horses at home. At high-end stables in the Northeast and California, monthly fees for training, housing and feeding can reach $2,500 per horse. Part of that is attributed to rising agriculture prices, with oat prices up 14% from 2013 through July 2014 and alfalfa-hay prices up 5% in the same period.

Stables. Its all well and good buying a property with a large patch of land for your horses, but you will also have to keep them in suitable stables. A property complete with stables will probably have a higher asking price, but it could save you a lot of money and hassle in the long run. Even small stables can cost thousands of dollars to construct, and larger stables can cost hundreds of thousands. If there are no stables, you may have to get planning permission to erect them yourself, so always find out whether this is going to pose any difficulties before you invest in a property.

Land Requirements. You are going to need a decent amount of land to look after a horse properly. How much exactly? The answer depends on whether the pasture is of a high quality and how many horses you have and their size. However, as a general guide, aim for at least 1 acre of land per small horse, but preferably more. Depending on where you purchase in the country, pasture might not be an option. Also, make sure you plan ahead. You may want to keep more horses on your land in the future, and you will need to think about this in advance to avoid having to sell again a few years down the line.

Location. You should also pay close attention to the location of the property in relation to nearby bridle paths/trails, riding schools and horse shows. If you plan to take your horses out regularly, then it is a good idea to reduce travel times as much as possible. You are going to need to take your horse out from time to time, so having suitable access to your property is essential. Will you be able to move your horses in and out of the property without any problems? If the driveway is not suitable, then this may require some work, and this can significantly add to your overall costs.

Fencing. Suitable fencing is vital, and this means fencing that is strong and high enough to keep your horses safely inside the area. Hedges are not the best idea because they take a long time to grow and are not as reliable. Wood, vinyl or pipe fences are a better option. Fencing the entire enclosure will be quite expensive, so make sure you are prepared for the costs involved. If you have a few acres of land, the cost can quickly rise to thousands of dollars and time spent.

Choose Your Equestrian Property with Care. Choosing an equestrian property is a decision that you should make very carefully. There is so much more involved in purchasing this type of property than a standard property, and there are many important factors to consider. Get your decision wrong, and you could find yourself spending a lot of money trying to rectify problems you should have spotted in the first place. If you have any doubts, it is best to work alongside an agent who has experience in the local area and equestrian properties to ensure the purchase goes as smoothly as possible.

> *There is something about the outside of a horse that is good for the inside of a man.*
> – Winston Churchill

Selling: If you can lead a horse to water…

How has the market affected your horse property's value? The first step is for you to become properly educated and have a clear understanding of your horse property's fair market value. You can select any agent to list your home on the MLS and hope that another agent brings you a buyer. This is called a "passive listing." In today's cut throat real estate market you need more than just a passive approach to not only sell your home but get you the absolute top dollar. You need someone that is a master at marketing and selling equestrian property. Your agent's website needs to parallel what shoppers are specifically looking for in horse property, and guides them directly to equestrian property that matches their search request. We use an "active approach" for our listings which means that we aggressively go after specific markets that target buyers who are looking to purchase the type of home you are selling.

Increased demand. There's strong demand for properties with land and stables. You cannot take for face value what self-generated value sites like Zillow, Trulia or even the tax assessor's office say your property is worth. The only accurate way is for a real estate professional that is familiar with your area to conduct a comparable market analysis that will advise you of your equestrian properties fair market value. Our market analysis compares horse properties, farms, ranches and equestrian estates inside & outside your neighborhood that have recently sold along with pending sales, expired listings and properties currently for sale. You will need someone that can accurately explain the adjustments of each comparable and educate you on how your property stacks up against the competition. Horse properties are like custom homes, no two are alike. Knowing the difference between barn companies and the resources they use to make their product can be the difference of thousands of dollars.

Competitively Pricing Your Horse Property. One of the most important issues you will face is pricing your home and property. Pricing will determine:

- How quickly your property sells

- How attractive your property will be to buyers

- How you will reach your financial goals regarding the transaction

Unless there are extenuating circumstances such as your property being located in a high-risk, undesirable or unusual area, the listing price of your property will set the tone for your entire transaction.

Key aspects to consider:

- How soon do I want to sell my property?

- Statistics show the narrower the gap between the asking price and my estimate of value, the sooner an offer will come in.

- What are buyers willing to offer?

Buyers are interested in your property's comparable worth, not what you might need to get out of the property. The buyer's perception of the value of your ranch will not be altered by the cost of your next home, your need to pay off an existing mortgage or your hope for a dollar-for-dollar return on ranch improvements. Remember that sellers and realtors are not appraisers, buyers are. In the end, it is the buyer's evaluation that matters. Buyers make their assessments by comparing your property with others that offer like features and are in a similar condition to yours.

Is there any harm in overpricing property? Yes. To effectively price your home, you must establish a solid correlation between the asking price and the fair market value. A realistic asking price will result in a fast, lucrative sale. If your price is out of sync with the market, you're likely to turn off a large group of potential buyers. Contrary to popular belief, a buyer usually makes an offer on a fairly priced property before making a lower offer on a listing that is seen as overpriced. Also, overpricing your equestrian property often helps sell your neighbor's property faster than yours.

But my horse facility is worth so much more. Emotion and pride should have no place in the pricing process. Sellers speak of the value, amount invested and what they can afford "to take." Buyers consider only price, condition and other properties offered.

Should I leave room for negotiating? Experience has shown that the closer your listing price is to the supporting comparable sales data, the greater your chances for a quick sale at or near your asking price. As a result, we recommend pricing as close to that figure as possible. If you list your property at an unreasonably high price and receive a full-priced offer, the price will be tested during the appraisal and lending process. As a result, it's important to price your property at something comparables and the experience of the local brokers can justify. In fact, many agents will miss showing your property to potentially qualified buyers simply because at face value your property is out of their clients' price range.

Winning Marketing Plan. The marketing goal should be to expose your horse property with the highest quality representation. Buyers have ranked photography as the most important feature on real estate websites and property brochures. Obtaining quality photography quickly should be the first priority of the listing process. Creating a compelling marketing plan and a brochure printed on heavy card stock paper should be a second initiative. With attention to narrative details, the "keywords" that are used to describe your property are what will help buyers find your property.

Rudy L. Kusuma

Marketing plan in detail:

- Price your home to be competitive in today's market
- Offer staging tips to make your property "Show Off"
- Professional photo shoot for online and in print advertising
- Professional "High Definition" virtual tour of your home
- Advertise your listing worldwide
- Optimizing your home's visibility on over 300 syndicated real estate websites
- Featuring your property on a search engine optimized real estate website
- Expose your property to over 30,000 network agents
- Analyzing our personal realty database for buyers looking for a property like yours
- Attract thousands of qualified buyers to view your property
- Convert these shoppers into showings
- Electronic lock box and online showing requests to track all agent activity
- Presenting all offers and explaining the pros and cons to assist you in making educated choices
- Negotiate on your behalf the best possible terms and price for your home
- Facilitating the transaction from contract to close with no surprises
- Qualified agent: Horses are not our whole lives but they make our lives whole

Benefits of working with an equestrian property specialist. A qualified, competent real estate agent will help you navigate the myriad of decisions that arise when buying and selling a home. An agent provides value to the homeowner in many ways:

- Offers seller guarantees in writing

- Adds experience and expertise in all aspects of the sales process including marketing, financing, negotiations and more

- Handles all showings

- Has a network of known, trusted real estate professionals. If your agent doesn't have the answer, he or she likely knows someone who does

- Always have your interests in mind, so you always have someone on your side

- Can handle and advise on all price and contract negotiations

- Provides you with all the possible options and opportunities without holding back

- Gives an unbiased, realistic view of your home and your options. Unlike buyers and sellers, an agent has no emotional attachment to property

- Has the knowledge to help you ask the right questions

- Being a third party, potential buyers are more likely to tell your agent the truth about your home even if it is unflattering. This objective viewpoint will help you make the necessary changes to get your home sold

- Your time is valuable. By hiring a real estate agent it allows you to spend your time how you want, rather than being tied down with the marketing and showing appointments of your home.

One principle of marketing is the use of exclusivity. A good agent will understand how to market a property with some exclusivity in a way that has buyers clamoring to know more.

TWELVE

Buyer Profile Systems

By Sarah Grimm

Not all real estate agents invest their time and resources in becoming masters of their craft, that craft being the selling of your home. What is more, many real estate agents don't understand the basic principles of marketing and their expertise stops at pounding a for sale sign in your yard. As a home seller, their lack of skill and training can result in your home taking longer to sell, for less money, or, even worse, your home could not sell at all! What should you do to avoid getting stuck with one of these under qualified agents? Ask questions! How can you determine if an agent is qualified to sell your home or not? What questions should you ask to satisfy yourself that you are hiring a true marketing professional? While, there are many questions that you can ask agents that will help you determine their skill level, there is really one that will tell you all that you need to know: How are you going to find a buyer for my home?

Does your Agent have Buyers?

Any agent worth their salt spends a significant amount of time, energy and money in their real estate business finding buyers for homes that they don't even have for sale yet. Why would an agent do that? For the simple reason that good agents know that a home seller needs a home buyer for the sale to take place. Every top notch real estate agent that we have ever come across has a database full of what our office calls "Buyers in Waiting." These are people who are serious home buyers, but are not currently active in the marketplace for various reasons. For some, the timing isn't right, for others they just haven't found "THE" home that makes them want to move. Whatever their reason for not moving, it is possible that one of these individuals could be the buyer for your home. Your home could already be sold! Ask a potential agent how many buyers he or she has in their database and ask for proof. Most agents will not have the ability to show you their "Buyers In Waiting" list on the spot. If you ask for that list, one of two things will usually happen. One, the agent with buyers will give you a number and tell you that they will send you a list of these buyers. The second agent, with no buyers will hem and haw and perhaps even look confused by your question. This agent is dangerous to your pocketbook. Think very carefully before hiring this type of agent! If an agent pulls out this list when you ask, hire that person right away. That is an agent who understands basic marketing!

Where do Buyers Come From?

Another tool of a successful agent is to understand where buyers come from. Over the last decade, buyers have begun their home search on the internet in rapidly increasing numbers. It is vital that a professional agent have a strong online presence. Our real estate team has three main websites we utilize to draw buyers and countless others with whom we have some presence. However, keep in mind that many agents have flashy websites that have lots of bells and whistles, but they do nothing to capture potential buyers and just serve to satisfy the ego of the agent. How can you know? Again, ask. Ask your agent how he or she collects buyers for potential homes. Keep in mind the internet should only be one source of buyer collection. A good agent should have at least three ways to draw buyers into their database; a GREAT Agent will have at least five!

Does your Agent do any Pre-Marketing?

One principle of marketing is the use of exclusivity. A good agent will understand how to market a property with some exclusivity in a way that has buyers clamoring to know more. I will give you an example: I am not a big shopper. In fact, if I can order something online and have it shipped to my house and I never have to darken the doorway of the mall, I am happy. I also hate to have store credit cards for a variety reasons. One reason is they have very high interest rates. However, one day I found myself with my mother at Nordstrom picking up items as gifts for my nephews. I noticed that Nordstrom had hung a large curtain up behind the register, and only a few patrons were being allowed to enter the area behind the curtain. Of course, my curiosity got the best of me and I had to know what these lucky people were getting access to and how I could get in as well. The short answer was and is if you have a Nordstrom Credit or Debit card, you get early access to Anniversary sale items and prices several days before they go on the market to the general public. Not only do these Nordstrom shoppers get early access to the best deals and the hottest new products, but they get to be a VIP when they do it. That is exclusivity! If you are wondering, I did get a Nordstrom credit card and I am now one of the lucky few who get to buy my kids' school shoes at the end of every July at a discount before the general population has a chance to snatch them up. The same basic principle can be applied to housing. Buyers know good houses sell very quickly. They need to know that they are working with an agent that will give them priority access to proprietary information. Ask your potential agent, "do you do any pre-marketing? If so what?" Our team has a 50 step pre-marketing plan designed to drum up as much potential interest about your home before it hits the MLS. Could your home be sold before it even hits the market? It is possible as we have been able to help many of our sellers spend less than 24 hours on the market, many without ever hitting the market, by effective use of the principle of exclusivity. Our sellers are happy because they only had to show their home for a few hours and buyers are happy because they beat out everyone else.

Now that my house is on the Market where are you going to find my Buyer?

It is not uncommon for sellers to need or want their home on the market right away, and a pre-marketing period is not possible. However, that does not mean that a real estate agent can stop their buyer profile activities. Good agents know their data. What are the statistics and demographics in the neighborhood? Have the buyers in your neighborhood in the last 12 months consisted of mostly families? Have professionals or young hipsters found that your neighborhood is the place to be? This kind of information is available to the public, and can leave clues as to who your buyer is likely to be. Ask your agent, "What are the demographics of my neighborhood? Who is currently buying in my neighborhood?" Most importantly, ask "How are you going to reach those buyers?"

Real estate agents should represent more than a cheesy card, a flashy car and big hair.

Selling homes is an imperfect science because markets are made up of people, and people change. What is more, the market is ever shifting and moving. You owe it to yourself to partner with a real estate agent, who understands and closely monitors these changes. Market knowledge is essential. Understanding of marketing principles is crucial. Find an agent who knows how to get buyers!

When a client can start to perceive the contractual process as more than the ink that's written on paper, it opens up a world of possibilities to help put deals together that may otherwise never have a chance at life.

THIRTEEN

Contracts

By Adam Kutchuk

I have a bit of a confession to make: I enjoy contracts. I know that makes me a bit of a strange animal, and I'm ok with that. Back in my law school days, my fellow students dreaded the heavy workload of our "contract" classes. I loved them. I can only speak for myself, but before I enrolled in my contract classes, my perception of a contract was that it required to be an official government form with strong legal wording, and other arcane qualities that would make it legally enforceable in a court of law. This could not be further from the truth.

Before I go any further, it's important to mention that I am not a lawyer, and I cannot give legal advice. I only have the life benefit of going to law school, and that provides me with an educated perspective/experience on the contractual process.

According to Wikipedia, this is the definition of a contract:

> *In common law legal systems, a contract (or informally known as an agreement in some jurisdictions) is an agreement having a lawful object entered into voluntarily by two or more parties, each of whom intends to create one or more legal obligations between them. The elements of a contract are "offer" and "acceptance" by "competent persons" having legal capacity who exchange "consideration" to create "mutuality of obligation.*

To make that sound more like common conversation, in essence that says the contract is something that two people agree upon where each person gains something and also gives up something, and is legally enforceable. Isn't that a lot easier to swallow? I always felt that law school was full of wordy legalese that was intended to confuse the general public and encourage their reliance on the law community.

Contract: an agreement that is binding on the weaker party.
-Frederick Sawyer

One of the first cases we read about involved two parties (Lucy v. Zehmer) in a bar that had a conversation about buying and selling a farm for $50,000. This was much less than the property was truly worth. They came to an agreement on price, wrote it down on a bar napkin, and signed it. As I was reading this case, I remember thinking "That can't be enforceable. It must be on a government blessed magically rendered contract to be legal." Now I won't bore you with all the legal elements of that particular case, but in the end, it was a legal and enforceable contract.

How can a bar napkin be legally enforceable?? I had asked about this in the following class session, and my professor's reply was something I'll never forget. He said, "You can paint your contract on the side of a cow, and as long as all of the legal elements are met, it is enforceable." I tuned out for a few minutes and thought about selling my next property via bovine contract. That opportunity has not presented itself in my 14-year real estate career, however, I'm not giving up hope.

Since this is a real estate book, it's important this information loop back to the real estate process. At some point in time, your real estate transaction is going to arrive at the contractual phase. A question that is rarely asked by both buyers and sellers is "How well do you understand the contractual process?" People typically ask:

- How many houses did you sell this year?

- How many buyers do you have in your pipeline?

- What type of marketing does your company provide?

- What is your commission structure?

The extremely critical element of "How well do you know the contractual part of real estate" is rarely discussed. I encourage you to ask your next real estate professional this direct question. Ask them if they have contractual strategies that go above and beyond what a typical agent can provide. Any competent agent can fill in the blanks on a standard purchase contract, however, an elite agent should be able to provide you with some competitive contractual advantages as he/she is representing your interests.

A basic conversation that I have with all of my clients up front is that a contract can be anything that two people are willing to agree upon. I like to use the following example to get my clients thinking out of the box:

Adam- *Mr. Buyer, did you know that there is a Miscellaneous section in the contract where we can add anything we want to the contract.*

Buyer- *No, I was not aware of that.*

Adam- *Yes, there is. For example, we can write in there that you are willing to pay full price for this home on the condition that the seller comeback every other Tuesday to wash your car for the next six months.*

Buyer- *That sounds ridiculous and can't possibly be enforceable.*

Adam- *Actually, as long as you both agree to it, and sign the contract, it's not ridiculous at all and it becomes an enforceable element of the contract.*

When a client can start to perceive the contractual process as more than the ink that's written on paper, it opens up a world of possibilities to help put deals together that may otherwise never have a chance at life.

Let's say that you are working with a client that does not have a lot of cash to work with, and he certainly cannot afford to put down an initial deposit on a property ($1,000- $10,000). Most agents would be dead in the water at that point. Did you know that the initial deposit does not have to be cash? For a contract to be legal, the consideration or initial deposit simply has to be something of value. A creative contract can be written like this:

Joe Smith offers to purchase your property for $100,000. He will make an initial deposit of $100 and hand over title of his 2007 Nissan Sentra valued at $5,000. Seller to carry back the balance of $94,900. Payments to be made monthly at...

As long as the buyer and seller agree to these terms, a contract is created.

Rudy L. Kusuma

Buyers!

Do not be afraid to be creative and powerful with your offers. If you are in a competitive situation and you are offering your absolute maximum as far as what you financially qualify for, have your agent throw in something that your life skills can offer. If you're a mechanic, offer free oil changes for six months, if you're a baker offer free pies every week for a year. Do something that might not cost a whole lot, while at the same time offers perceived value that makes your offer a bit stronger and unique compared to the other black and white offers on the table.

You may be inclined to say, "Adam, I have the most boring job known to man. It provides no services, goods, or anything of value to the general population." then I'm sorry, but I still have a potential solution for you. Buy year round tickets to Disneyland or some local attraction. Consider the psychological effect that has when your offer is presented side by side to a basic vanilla contract. In a competitive market like our Southern California market, this has had a tremendous impact in my experience. Little, creative elements like that can lead you to contract victory!

I know it's impossible to be an expert at contracts after reading a few short pages on such a deep topic. However, I hope that I have challenged your perspectives on what a contract is, and what it can be. I wish you luck on your next negotiation! If you happen to have an awesome contractual story, I'd love to hear about it. Email me at Adam@realtyWRKS.com and put "My Creative Contract Story" in the subject line. Maybe it will get in my next book.

FOURTEEN

Don't Sell Your House More than Once

By John Gluch

So your house has been on the market for what seems like 972 days even though it's been one week and you see your real estate agent's name pop up on your phone. You answer, hopeful and expectant. Will this be the day? Will this be the day that you have waited for these long seven days as people came in and out of your house? Will this be that fateful day when you receive your very first offer? Sure enough, you pick up the phone, and your agent's tone is even more positive than normal. "Mr. Johnson I have wonderful news for you, we have received an offer on your home and it's a full price offer!" Before your agent can even finish his sentence you begin jumping up and down, dancing around the living room. You pick up your 6-month-old baby and throw her in the air exclaiming "we are rich, we are rich!" and expect that at any moment the new buyer's bank will arrive with an armored car full of gold coins to drop off at your front door. Now you can finally buy that new home you have been eyeing on the other side of town! Just moments after you promise your next born child to your agent as a thank you for his amazing work he breaks the news. "Mr. Johnson lets pump the brakes just a bit here. While this is a wonderful first step, we still have lots of work to do. The buyer is very excited to purchase your home but between here and the finish line we have several hurdles to clear. Why don't you put your daughter back in the crib and I'll talk you through the next few steps?"

Yes, it's true; that first offer is a beautiful site to see but the truth is that lots of real estate contracts fall apart before they close and that puts you as the seller back to square one. Now, instead of handing over your keys to the new owners of your home you are back to showing your house over and over again, waiting and hoping that the next buyer will come along soon. This chapter is written to prevent all of that and ensure that the first offer you accept ends up being the one that closes!

Remember Who's in Charge

As a seller, it's very important to remember that most purchase contracts are worded to give the buyers several ways out of the contract and the sellers very few ways out. This makes sense as the buyers are taking on all of the risks associated with making a huge purchase. That said since you have very few ways out, and the buyers have so many it is wise as a seller to be picky about whom you accept an offer from. You want to do your best to minimize the chances that the buyers you sign on the dotted line with will cancel on you. There are three basic issues you will want to address on the front end of every offer: Buyer motivation, ability to obtain financing and potential contractual challenges.

Buyer Motivation

How badly does the buyer want your house? Perhaps this is the most important question that can be asked. We have all heard the tales of mothers lifting automobiles up off of the ground to save their children from auto accidents. What you want is a buyer who will do anything to buy your house! In the world of real estate, this translates into a buyer who has a real and urgent need to buy and specific reasons why your house is the one for them. Have your agent dig into these questions with the buyer's agent. At the bottom of the motivation spectrum, you will find investors wanting to buy your home as a rental. In hot markets, investors will write offers on houses they have not even seen only to cancel when they do finally get a chance to see it. What you want is a person who really spent some time in the home, brought a measuring tape and a camera and took it all in. You want a family who, after much consideration, has determined that they just cannot live anywhere else; they absolutely need to purchase to your home.

Now of course I have drawn some extreme pictures here and, to be frank, not all homes will elicit the high levels of motivation explained here. Homes in desperate need of a remodel, overpriced, or in undesirable locations may receive few if any offers and in some cases you are best to accept anything you can get. That said, whenever possible you will want to get a good gauge for the excitement level of your potential buyers

Here is a list of questions to help you determine the interest of your buyer:

- Has your buyer seen the home and if so how many times?

- How long were they in the home when they viewed it?

- On a scale of 1-10, how excited are the buyers about your home?

- Has your buyer been under contract with other homes and then cancelled? This question helps you feel out if these are the types of buyers who have made a habit of canceling contracts during escrow.

- How long has the buyer's agent known the buyers? The longer the relationship, the more valuable the agents insights into his buyers.

- How many homes has the agent sold this year? A good, active agent will be much better at managing his time and will be less likely to waste your time with an unmotivated buyer.

Contractual Contingencies

All purchase contracts will have various ways for the buyer to get out of the deal. These "outs" are called contingencies and what the contract is stating is that the buyer will purchase the home contingent upon X, Y, and Z. While each contract will differ we will address the three major contingencies found in most purchase contracts: Inspection, Appraisal, and Financing.

Inspection Contingency (AKA the Due Diligence Period)

Most home purchases will be contingent upon the buyer's performance of various inspections and investigations that they are permitted to perform over a specific, stated period. In Arizona, inspection periods are most commonly ten days. During those ten days, buyers will typically have a licensed home inspector and perhaps various other specific licensed contractors view the home and report back as to its condition. The buyer then gives the seller notice of any items she has uncovered that she objects to and either A) cancels the purchase of the home B) gives the seller a chance to correct the objected to items or C) elects to move ahead with the purchase and takes the property as is. In Arizona, as in many other areas, the buyer can effectively cancel just based on a change of heart. In other words, the reason they are canceling does not need to meet some objective standard of being a "good enough" reason to cancel. Here are some ways of minimizing the chances the seller will cancel on you during this inspection period:

- Gauge motivation. A motivated buyer can "live" with a lot more than an unmotivated one.

- Have a home inspection prior to listing your home and do your best to fix the items uncovered by the inspector.

- Disclose to the buyer everything negative you know about the home before signing a contract with them. This serves two purposes. One is that it makes it unlikely they will cancel based on the revelation of those items, and the other is it removes those items as negotiating points down the road for any items you are unwilling to fix e.g. if the roof is old and in need of replacement and you are unwilling to do the needed work. By disclosing this on the front end, it is less likely that the buyer comes to you during the inspection period asking for roof replacement or a reduction in price because of the old roof.

- Shorten the inspection period. In my experience this is an easy ask and most people will easily agree to seven days as opposed to ten or whatever is customary in your area. If you stand on good footing in the negotiation, ask for this period to be shortened.

- No doesn't mean no. I have saved lots of deals by simply not taking no as an answer. If a buyer inspects your home and cancels because of condition issues, do your best to let them know of your willingness to address those issues. Some buyers just get nervous and overwhelmed. Do your best to let them know you will take care of their major concerns and often times you can keep them at the negotiation table.

- Offer a home warranty. If you have not already done so, offer a home warranty to cover some of the buyer's bigger concerns. This is especially helpful in the case of older but working items like an old air conditioner. A home warranty will cover older items like this should they break down the road and can often keep a deal together.

Appraisal Contingency

All conventional banks will require that your buyer obtain an appraisal from a neutral third party. This appraiser will give his opinion of value and assure the bank that your buyer is not overpaying for the home. In the majority of cases appraised values come in at exactly the same number as the purchase price. In other words, if your contract price is $250,000 then most likely the appraised value will be the same. If the appraised value comes in higher than the purchase price then, nothing changes and the buyer moves ahead with the purchase. However, if the appraised value comes in lower than the purchase price the buyer then has the option to cancel the contract. Low appraisals are one of the hardest things to predict and most challenging to overcome but here are some tips on clearing this hurdle.

- Ask the buyer to waive the appraisal contingency. This is a big ask but if you have multiple offers or an exceptionally high demand home you may be able to get the buyer to waive his right to cancel based on a low appraisal.

- Have your agent provide the appraiser with comparable sales that justify your price. If none are available, keep in mind that appraisal may become an issue.

- Ask that the appraisal be ordered quickly. Some contracts do not specifically stipulate when an appraisal should be ordered. Negotiate up front that it be ordered right away so that if it does come in low you can address it immediately rather than getting surprised late in the game.

- Provide the appraiser with a simple list of upgrades you have done to the home in the past five years. Not all of the upgrades will be self-evident; you want to demonstrate to the appraiser that your home is better than the rest.

- If the appraisal comes in low, ask the buyer to make up the difference or meet you half way. Low appraisals don't have to kill the deal. If the seller has enough extra cash to make up the difference between appraised value and purchase price in cash then, the deal is still alive. Alternatively, you might meet them in the middle. Offer to decrease the price by half of the difference and ask them to bring extra cash to the table for the other half.

Ability to Obtain Financing

One way or another, your buyer will have to track down the funds to purchase your home. There are more and less desirable sources for those funds ranging anywhere from a cash buyer to a buyer selling his collection of baseball cards to pay for your home. Regardless of the financing type, here are some steps you can take to be sure your buyer does not show up to the closing table empty handed.

Financed Offers

Most purchase contracts will be contingent upon the buyer's obtaining financing via a conventional lending institution like a bank or mortgage broker. Require that the buyer provide an official pre-qualification form from his lender verifying that he is indeed qualified to be approved for a loan. Most lenders do a thorough job qualifying buyers to be absolutely sure that short of a big surprise (like a buyer losing a job during the purchase) the buyers they represent can indeed get a loan. Still, you should not rely entirely on the lender to qualify your prospective buyer. Here are some questions to ask your buyers lender.

- If the appraisal comes in low does the buyer have cash to make up the difference?

- Does the buyer currently have funds available for their down payment and closing costs or are they saving for it/borrowing it?

- Did the lender pull the buyer's credit? How does it look?

- Is the borrower self-employed or commissioned? These loans require two years tax returns. Did the lender collect those or take the borrowers word for it?

- Is the buyer selling their current home?

- Did the lender run desktop underwriter? If not why? This is a program a lender will use to pre-qualify buyers and if they were approved via this system it is more likely they will not have financing issues down the road.

- Are there any issues at all with getting this buyer financed?

- How long have you been in the business of lending and how many loans do you do a year? Experience is vital, and the more seasoned the lender, the more likely things will go well.

Cash

As they say, cash is king. Cash offers are the best possible offer from a financing perspective because the buyers are not relying on a bank to give them the thumbs up on buying your home. There are some specific details you will want to investigate with cash offers as all cash offers are not to be treated equally.

- Ask for proof of funds in order to verify that the buyer really does have the money. This can come in the form of a signed and dated letter from the buyer's banker or investment advisor, a screen shot of a similar account, or some other official form demonstrating the actual possession of the needed funds.

- If the account is in the name of a business or some other person, obtain a signed letter from the owner of that entity explaining the availability of the funds and giving the buyer permission to use them as they desire.

- Is the buyer still getting an appraisal? Unless the contract specifies that the buyer is not utilizing the appraisal contingency then it may still exist in the contract. Be sure to clarify this.

While you can never know with certainty that your new buyer will go the distance on your home purchase, following these guidelines will make it much more likely that they do. Trust your agent and her advice as well. Each contract has its own nuances and specific details that a trusted expert will help you evaluate on a case by case basis. With the help of a good agent, your home sale will close on time, and you'll only have to sell it once!

Don't profile the buyer. The ad should not focus directly on a particular group of people. Look at every financially qualified person as a probable buyer.

FIFTEEN

How to Write Classified Ads That Sell Homes

By Ahmad Shalforoshzadeh

As realtors, writing ad copy for newspapers, brochures and internet sites is part of our everyday life. One of the greatest skills we can acquire is how to write in a compelling way. Our goal is to create a positive impression of a property and intrigue a potential buyer by writing a classified real estate ad that includes descriptive information, attention-grabbing language and contact information for the owner or agent. More so, we must be vigilant so our property descriptions are accurate, precise as well as in compliance with Fair Housing laws.

Which of the below ads would you prefer to read?

For Sale: 3 Bedroom, 2 bath home with large living area and kitchen. Recently updated and in a good neighborhood.

or

You have to see this spacious 3 bedroom, 2 bath home in the prestigious Lockwood Estates neighborhood! Quality finishes throughout as this home has been lovingly updated with new flooring, paint and fixtures. No detail has been overlooked from the high-end stainless steel kitchen appliances to the crown molding accents. Ready to move in and enjoy for the new school year.

My guess is that you would more than likely become intrigued with how the second version of the ad is written as opposed to the first. You can take an average home and turn it into the Taj Mahal just by the use of descriptive words. Add in great photos, an eye catching ad title, and you have a terrific way to present a listing.

12 Things to Consider

1. **Know your audience.** Consider different marketing mediums such as a custom web page, magazine, newspaper, and brochures. It all depends on your target audience. Surely you will want to reach potential buyers as well as their agents and brokers.

2. **Write a headline that will grab attention.** The headline should be an attention grabber and stand out. Use words that appeal to your audience.

3. **Highlight the best parts of the house or property.** Always be meticulous to outline the features of the property. Don't profile the buyer. The ad should not focus directly on a particular group of people. Look at every financially qualified person as a probable buyer. For example, if you are selling a small townhouse, you don't want to advertise it as the perfect bachelor pad. Doing so may dissuade a newlywed couple from showing interest in it because of the bachelor pad label.

Here some examples that describe the property:

- Charming craftsman style home with wide front porch

- Condo with fully furnished exercise center and pool

- Fireplace in the cozy den

- Take a break from yard work

- Enjoy your own private resort

Avoid phrases such as these that focus on the buyer:

- Empty nesters welcome. *Are kids not welcome?*

- Great family neighborhood. *Will a single person feel awkward?*

- Near Indian grocery. *Is this the Indian part of town?*

- Perfect for single guy. *Is it safe for other people?*

- Bring your kids. *Sorry, don't have any!*

4. **Ad copy conveys a sense of the neighborhood as well as the home itself.**

    Here are some phrases that describe the community:

    - Gated neighborhood

    - Estate-sized lots

    - Popular neighborhood close to shopping

    - Secluded setting

    - 1940's era neighborhood

    - On the golf course

5. **Avoid phrases that focus on the neighbors themselves.** It is one thing to talk about the neighborhood and another thing to talk about the neighbors. Never indicate a preference for certain types of people to the exclusion of others.

    Stay away from these kinds of phrases:

    - Exclusive area. *Who is excluded?*

    - Executive level home. *What about middle management?*

    - Elite neighborhood. *Who qualifies?*

    - Country club area. *Are non-members allowed?*

- Neighborhood of young families. *What about older folks?*

- Quiet, conservative neighborhood

6. **Avoid the use of brand names in a generic way.** If you use a brand name, make sure the item is that brand.

   Here are some common mistakes:

   - Jacuzzi tub
   - Corian counters
   - Andersen windows
   - Sub-Zero refrigerator

7. **Do not offer assurances about what can be done with the property.** Adding on may be more difficult than you realize. Basements on the property, deed restrictions, soil conditions, neighborhood opposition or building ordinances may be obstacles to construction. The buyer may rely on your offhand statement, and be very disappointed later.

   Avoid statements like these:

   - Plenty of room for a pool
   - Ready for new master bedroom
   - Add a second story and see downtown
   - Sub-divide, and have two lots
   - Perfect for bed and breakfast
   - Unobstructed view of the lake

8. **Provide a call to action.** You want your readers to do something after they read the ad, so make sure you are clear about what they should do.

   - Leave a phone number if you want people to call you.

   - Include an email address or website if you want people to contact you electronically. If running a classified real estate ad online, place a link in the ad that will take viewers directly to your website or your email address.

   - Details about any open houses or scheduled visits. Invite people to visit the property by leaving the address as well as the date and time they are welcome to view it.

9. **Include any additional contact information.** This might be the selling agent's name, the property manager's information or set up a recorded hotline that people can call for additional information.

10. **Provide photos.** Pictures will heighten the interest of the ad. If you have the budget to purchase extra ad space, including one or two photos of the exterior and interior is a great idea.

    - Consider a virtual tour. This is helpful when the classified ad is online and able to link to other sites.

11. **Use relevant keywords when you are listing the ad online.** Whether utilizing a free site such as Craigslist, an online newspaper or the Multiple Listing Service (MLS), keywords are essential to driving traffic to your ad when people search the internet.

12. **Link to applicable maps and directions when writing an online classified ad.**

Magazine Advertising

Magazine ads are not likely to produce an immediate buyer. Lead-time is the difficulty. The home ad submitted today might not make it to someone's doorstep for 30 to 60 days, sometimes even longer. In reality, the ad will be stuck in the back and ignored as the recipient flips through a couple articles before tossing the magazine into a recycling bin. Very few magazines are re-read because of the time sensitive nature. If your home is advertised in the August edition of the homes magazine then who's to say that it won't have a price reduction or be sold the following month and the reader can just pick up the next month's edition to see the hottest new properties.

Newspaper Advertising

A local weekly paper might be a better place to advertise a home for sale. But the ad copy should stand out and be well designed to attract attention. Local, daily and weekly newspaper readership is declining, but in a few markets, it's still a desired place to advertise a home for sale. Even non-subscribers might buy a Sunday newspaper to look at the ads of homes for sale. Before placing a newspaper ad, get a copy of the paper. If nobody else is advertising, don't waste the money on a newspaper ad.

Direct Mail

You can purchase specific mailing lists by identifying the characteristics of the potential. Look for direct mail list brokers in the Yellow Pages. Printing companies that offer direct mail services are also good sources for this information.

Internet Advertising

Statistics show that 90% of all home searches are initiated online. By far, the most popular site is Realtor.com, probably because it's the easiest to remember. Many newspapers subscribe to local MLS feeds and download the latest home listings online.

Through popular internet sites such as vFlyer, Point2 and Postlets, online ads can be created instantly and for free. These websites will also post them on dozens of other frequently visited sites.

SIXTEEN

Marketing: Internet Based Effectiveness

By Nancy Braun

Four sites—Redfin and Zillow (Z)… Trulia (TRLA) and Realtor.com…—attract 61 million of the 67 million visitors to real estate websites each month in the U.S., according to ComScore (SCOR). They also generate hundreds of millions in revenue and have helped turn buying a house into entertainment—a spectator sport that can be enjoyed without darting surreptitiously into random open houses. Ninety percent of consumers now start their real estate journeys on the Web, according to the National Association of Realtors."
- Stone, Brad "Why Redfin, Zillow, and Trulia Haven't Killed Off Real Estate Brokers" Bloomberg BusinessWeek, March 7, 2013

I formed my company, Showcase Realty, LLC, in 2008 after holding my license with a large real estate office in Charlotte, North Carolina for 12 years. That firm had been selling real estate the same way for over 45 years. I knew that the internet was becoming more and more integral in our daily lives and that my company would need to adapt to the changes in the way real estate was being marketed. Showcase opened with one full-time assistant and a part-time bookkeeper. Very soon thereafter I brought on a full-time marketing professional recognizing that this would be the key to growth. As my company grew and experienced changes over the years, I always staffed the marketing department with talented and creative professionals.

From the beginning, I recognized that we needed to have a strong internet presence. Since many of the local companies in Charlotte had not recognized this need, we were able to create a very strong internet presence, and our listings were landing on the first page of the Google search engine results. Our SEO (search engine optimization) was very strong for a small startup company.

I always supported our marketing team's initiatives and was (and continue to be) open to trying new strategies. As the electronic presence of Showcase grew, I was invited to speak at real estate conferences and host webinars focusing on internet marketing for real estate professionals. Our initiatives were regarded as being on the cutting edge, and I started to gain many followers in the industry. The audience would inquire how I was able to implement our initiatives, and I would say, "I hire the talent to do this for our company." While, I support my team financially, come up with some of the ideas myself and engage consultants to guide them, I cannot take credit for these creative initiatives. Having a creative team in place along with the financial support makes a difference.

With the recent purchase of Trulia, Zillow is strengthening its market share of the real estate business on the internet. This is all the more reason to have a strong internet presence including the use of Trulia and Zillow.

I am a Premier Broker on Zillow and a Pro Broker on Trulia. There are also many other online tools of which we take advantage. We use Pay Per Click (PPC) to increase our online traffic and ultimately increase our lead generation. With our online presence and our lead coordination system, we now have over 5,000 leads in our database. We changed our websites, so they are WordPress based as Google prefers this over the template websites. Our sites are also mobile friendly. We are regularly posting on our blog, Twitter, LinkedIn, Google+, YouTube and Facebook. We post our listings on over 900 portals, and our luxury listings are posted on International sites as well as Wall Street Journal, New York Times and many other prestigious online sites. I contribute articles to various other trade publications and am quoted or written about in numerous magazines and newspapers. These in turn are posted on our website's Media Page. The underlying premise of everything we do is to offer information, rather than to sell. Our online objective is to be the go-to resource for questions about real estate.

Recognizing that people are reading less and watching more, the benefits of video are integral to online marketing. We have a professional videographer on our team and create unique and informative videos on relevant real estate matters and custom videos of our inventory and the neighborhoods we service. Our podcast, HowstheMarketRadio.com offers recordings of our radio show (How's the Market) which airs on a major News Talk radio station. It has been receiving over 1,000 downloads per show and listeners are invited to download free eBooks and reports on various real estate issues.

We have various WordPress based web pages linked to our main website as well as a "less branded" website to attract the prospect not looking for an agent, but instead just information on the home buying or selling process. We track all of our initiatives with Google analytics.

Our property signs all have descriptive URL's to entice the interested prospect to go to the internet to get more information about one of our programs. For example, our signs may say 704getyourprice.com, 704moveup.com, or paycashforyourhome.net. These all go to free e-reports and capture contact information (squeeze page).

Our internet presence has resulted in high name recognition (branding) and results-driven marketing. We have been #1 for lowest days on the market in my MLS, the highest percentage of list-to-sold price and have awesome lead capturing and conversion so that we sell our inventory quicker and for more money, and our agents are some of the most successful agents in the city.

We have embraced the internet and focus most of our marketing efforts on the internet. Its wide and diverse audience brings us traffic that ultimately converts to sales.

Buyers and sellers do their research online. Clients will check out the agent before initiating contact or even committing. This includes viewing the agent's social platforms and blogs

SEVENTEEN

Blogging and Content Marketing Strategy

By Nancy Braun

Today's marketing strategy must include blogging. Blogging is being part of the online conversation so your voice can serve as a resource tool. It needs to be at the center of any social media strategy. Blogs are easily searchable and often serve as a source of information, a modern day encyclopedia if you will. The content of the blog must be rich, authentic, consistently updated and of value to the consumer.

Many blogs are initiated with good intentions and then fall to the wayside when many get caught up with more pressing issues. If a consumer checks out the blog and sees that the content is not frequently updated, the value added is diminished. As an example, our blog would experience this during hectic times at our office, so we implemented a strategy to generate regular postings. We post market updates and media postings when quoted or referenced in the news. In addition, we decided to capitalize on our radio show, which airs weekly. After every recording of our show, we transcribe the show and then post segments in our blog. From there, we post snippets on various social media platforms. The blog is then regularly updated with authentic and relevant content.

7 Essential Elements Of A Good Blog

1. **Blog must be easy to read.** We live in a fast-paced culture and want the information we are seeking to be quick and concise. The best way to accomplish this is to have the blog highlighted with headlines and captions, and in addition effective keywords that are easily searched. The headline should clearly explain what the reader will receive when reading the blog. For example:

    • *5 staging tricks to get the highest price*

- *How to get your offer accepted when there are multiple offers*

- *Flip or hold for top Dollar$*

You no doubt have seen such sourced searches appear as part of internet search engines. These are information-based marketing links.

2. **Blog should include graphics, video and/or photos.** Pictures and graphics should tell a story and entice someone to read the blog for the content. Plain text can be dull and non-engaging at best.

3. **Offer an "opt in" to receive regular postings of your blog.** Invite the reader to automatically receive your posts via email. You want to create a following and be considered an "expert". Reading your blog just once will be easily forgotten. The reader should see your posts regularly and consistently.

4. **Snippets in your social media to draw your followers to your blog.** To increase your audience, share some of the blog's content in your social media platforms with links to the full blog. Attach a URL to the blog that describes what the blog is about. For example, *www.hudbuyersguide.com* or *www.6factsbeforeyoubuy.com*

5. **Share buttons.** Enable the blog readers to share the content to their social circles.

6. **Be relevant and do not sell!** The content should be of value and interesting to the reader. It should answer questions or enlighten the reader; it should not be a sales pitch. Content should be relevant to your target audience.

7. **Call to action.** Offer a free eBook or report on the subject discussed in the blog. This can be done with a squeeze page so you get the reader's contact information and follow up or put them on a drip campaign.

Content marketing is free. Many businesses spend a fortune on advertising with very little return. Content marketing serves many functions. It can capture the attention of new clients and also be affirming to a potential client. Buyers and sellers do their research online. Clients will check out the agent before initiating contact or even committing. This includes viewing the agent's social platforms and blogs. When I refer business to an agent outside of my service area, I will view their social media and website profiles and additionally checkout their blogs. If these platforms are outdated and poorly done, I move on to the next agent.

You have options. If you don't like to write or this is not your forte then hire someone to do this for you. You can even have an intern from a local college write copy. But if you outsource, be sure it is written as if you wrote it. Give the person some ideas and direction. And always, always review before publication or posting!

About The Authors

Nancy Braun

Nancy Braun is the creative force behind Charlotte, North Carolina's award-winning and innovative Showcase Realty, LLC. (www.showcaserealty.net) she founded the company in 2008 and quickly became a Certified Woman-Owned Business (WBENC & WOSB). In 2014, Nancy won the Charlotte Business Journal's "Women in Business Achievement Award".

Today, Nancy has successfully marketed and sold 1,000s of homes in Charlotte metro area. As a Top Producing Real Estate Broker, she expanded the company into divisions: Luxury Homes, Relocation Services, Residential Homes, Investment Properties, Property Management, and Short Sale and Foreclosure Services (representing HUD, national banking institutions, the City of Charlotte and numerous outsourcing companies). By focusing on innovation, attention to detail and creating a winning team of professionals, Nancy provides exceptional and professional service, personally delivered to her clients.

Nancy also hosts a weekly radio show, How's The Market: Real Estate. Real Answers Saturdays at 5 p.m. on 1110 WBT www.howsthemarketradio.com. She distributes a monthly real estate e-Newsletter, conducts monthly Realtor training workshops and is a speaker at National Trade Association Conferences and Webinars. Nancy is a member of the Force Advisory Board, Director of Public Relations, Dataflo MLS International REO North America and spokesperson of WinREO.

Nancy is a graduate of Cornell University and SUNY Buffalo School of Law and is also a member of BAR in New York and Washington, D.C. She was a recipient of the Dorothy B. Brothers Scholarship from the Women's Business Enterprise National Council and attended The Wharton School, University of Pennsylvania, Executive Education, Negotiations, 2014. Nancy is very passionate about her involvement with the Boys and Girls Club of Greater Charlotte and is on their Advisory Board and Chairperson of the Resource Development Executive Committee and a Member of REO4kids & REBSEA. Nancy is the proud mother of Jason (8 years old) and

Natalie (9 years old) and married to Mark Linch, who is an executive in the hotel business.

Sandy Casella

Sandy Casella bought her first home at the age of 22 with her husband. With no outside help from family members, Sandy and her husband learned the ropes of real estate investing, sometimes the hard way. Over the next several years, they bought several investment properties, flipping some of them and renting out the others. It was through this process that Sandy realized that not all real estate agents are created equally and that there were better ways to sell a home. Sandy originally obtained her real estate license in September 1989 in order to market her own investment properties. Several years later, she decided that selling real estate full time would be an exciting challenge. Sandy has been a top producing real estate ever since.

Sandy has always realized that there is a better way to do things and that the majority of ways in which real estate is marketed does not work, coupled with her insatiable desire to learn has caused her to seek out others who can teach her better methods. In August 2013, Sandy decided to join Craig Proctor Coaching to learn better ways to assist her clients in selling their most valuable asset as well as help them create wealth for themselves through real estate investing. Sandy realized instantly that being a part of this exclusive group was the right move and continues to learn from the best coaches and realtors in not only Canada but throughout North America and the World. These groups of real estate agents are unique in their approach, sharing idea's amongst themselves to continually raise the bar in their approach to new and innovative ways to market homes.

John Gluch

John Gluch wasn't born in Phoenix, but he got there as quick as he could! Now, just about 20 years later he loves the city so much that he has committed his career to helping people settle in. As a 2003 graduate from ASU with a Finance degree Mr. Gluch has helped hundreds of people buy, sell, and otherwise transition into the home of their dreams. While finance and numbers have always been his strong suit, the high rise office world just didn't have the same appeal that working with real life families did stated John. He loves his work and considers it a privilege to walk people through the largest investment most of them have ever made. Year after year John is consistently in the top ½ of 1% of real estate agents in Arizona and has built an incredible team of professionals that provide the very best in customer service. John Gluch loves meeting new people and has a passion for great meeting spots around town. Mr. Gluch be honored to meet with you and discuss your next move.

Sarah Grimm

Sarah Grimm is the Broker/Owner of Grimm & Associates at Metro Brokers in Denver, Colorado. In her 13 years as a professional Realtor, she has earned many awards for high production from her past Brokers, as well as her local Realtor Association. However, the designation she most values is the APREP designation that identifies her has one of the top 200 most trusted Real Estate Agents in North America and the press that she most treasures is the testimonials from past Clients who were happy and thankful to Sarah and her team for helping them accomplish their Real Estate goals.

Jared W. Jones

Known as the mega-agent of Las Vegas, Jared Jones has been a leading real estate investor, broker, and expert in Las Vegas for over a decade. He has sold over 3,000 homes in the Nevada market and has ranked in the top 5 agents in the nation by volume, out of a field of nearly 2 million Realtors.* Jones has helped many sellers gain high sales prices in a tough market, with many properties selling above asking price. With a home sale guarantee program, Jones offers sellers that they will have a guaranteed sale or they can keep 100% of his commission with no risk to the seller. In addition, the Jones Team has a full buyer database in place to help get properties sold quickly and for top dollar. Many Las Vegas area homebuyers have worked with Jones in order to find hard to find listings through foreclosures and off market homes.

Consistently ranking as one of the top agents in the state of Nevada and in the top tier of real estate agents nationwide, Jones has remained a force to be reckoned with even after the real estate market crash of 2008 with Las Vegas being one of the hardest hit areas in the country. Jared Jones is the CEO of Horizon Realty with locations in Las Vegas and Henderson, Nevada.

Rudy L. Kusuma

Rudy Kusuma is the Managing Director of TEAM NUVISION, Your REALTORS® Of Choice. He was recently selected as a Dave Ramsey Endorsed Local Provider (ELP) and enjoys consulting with San Gabriel Valley, California sellers and buyers with the heart of a teacher, not a salesperson. Rudy has been hosting a weekly real estate educational workshops for home buyers, sellers, and investors since 2007.

Rudy is the recipient of the 2013 and 2014 Five Star Real Estate Agent Award; this level of excellence is achieved by only less than 7% of the real estate agents in Southern California. Rudy has been recognized as the #1 Top Producer 2007 (ERA Arcadia office), 2008, 2009, 2010, 2011 (COLDWELL BANKER® San Gabriel office), and has been recognized as The Top Producer Team Leader of The Month 2012, 2013, 2014 (RE/MAX Alhambra office). Rudy and his team have sold over $100 Million in transactions and has been named among the top 200 Agents in the U.S. by the Accredited Platinum Real Estate Professionals Network.

As a philanthropist, Rudy is on a mission to raise $100,000 for the Children's Hospital in downtown Los Angeles. For every house that his team sells, Rudy and his team are donating a portion of their income to the Children's Hospital. Not only home sellers benefit from his team award winning service, but they donate a substantial portion of their income on every home sale to help the local children in the community.

Adam Kutchuk

Adam Kutchuk comes from a real estate family. Mr. Kutchuk's parents have been in real estate for over 30 years, and he now carries on the proud tradition of boring his kids to death with real estate stories at the dinner table. Adam went to middle school, high school, and delivered pizza in the same city of Temecula where he currently has his real estate company. Before Adam started his real estate career, he enlisted in the U.S. Marine Corps a few months out of high school. After that, Mr. Kutchuk was accepted into Pepperdine University, and graduated with a BA in Industrial/Organizational Psychology. At that point in life, he had to choose between being a fighter pilot and a real estate broker. Real estate won somehow, and it has lead to a wonderful career in residential real estate. Later in life, Adam went to Law school for a year and a half before going into the booming short sale market full time. Mr. Kutchuk has been in real estate for over 14 years now, and is a broker/owner with Realty Works in Temecula, Ca. He shares his office with his beautiful wife and that office shares a wall with his parent's office. Yes, he sees his family almost every day and that's not a bad thing!

Kirstin Kutchuk

Kirstin Kutchuk is dedicated to the marketing and sales of equestrian and luxury properties in Southern California. Kirstin has developed innovative marketing tools and contacts with people who are looking for a particular type of property. Having developed an appreciation for the true value of beautiful settings, Mrs. Kutchuk takes great pride in presenting unique places and properties. Kirstin consolidates area properties suitable for having horses (from backyard to state-of-the-art operations) and focuses on this property type. Unlike other real estate companies (and agents), her razor-sharp focus, knowledge of the inventory, and sensitivity to the equestrian; needs never go uncompromised. Her job is to assist buyers and sellers in reaching their goals in the least amount of time, with the fewest aggravations! And client advocacy is her number one goal, and that means that the client must be delighted with her service, and she must deliver beyond the clients expectations during the process. Kirstin Kutchuk loves what she does; she works hard, and takes great pleasure in providing excellent customer service! There is nothing better to Kirstin than a job well done.

As a passionate member of the "equestrian family," Kirstin Kutchuk has a desire to serve other "members" of this unique family. Aside from her career in horse management, breeding and equine studies, she has been riding since age 3 and a horse owner since age 11. She currently owns Quarter Horses on which she rides & shows in Reining competitions. Kirstin's diversified background in real estate, equestrian sports and equestrian studies have well prepared her for focusing on equestrian and luxury properties.

Jonathan Lahey

After graduating from the University of Maryland Baltimore County and graduating with a degree in Information Systems Management and Economics, Jonathan Lahey began not one but two careers. He worked as both an IT Consultant, as well as a realtor, specializing in condominiums, townhomes and single family homes.

An extremely hard worker, Jonathan was able to successfully juggle both jobs, but in 2008, he had to choose which one he would continue and which one he would have to leave behind. Luckily for the people in the Washington DC Metro area, Jonathan chose to continue his career in real estate.

Since choosing to focus on real estate, Jonathan has consistently finished in the top 1% in the nation as a realtor. In 2010, he was given the Re/Max Executive Club Award, and earned a 100% Club Award in both 2011 and 2012. In 2013, Jonathan earned the Platinum Award from Re/Max. Jonathan has also been designated as the top agent by the APREP and was selected as one of the Top Most Respected Real Estate Agents in North America. Currently, Jonathan is the leader of The Lahey Group that is comprised of nine superstar agents.

Ahmad Shalforoshzadeh

Ahmad Shalforoshzadeh grew up in Tehran where he started his business in the importing and exporting of auto parts. This business required from him high level of sales, negotiating, marketing, and management techniques, and this is where Ahmad improved and perfected this area. These skills followed him into his Real Estate business in 2005 where he started as an agent in Century 21. As of today, Ahmad is one of the top agents in Re/max and continues to grow and aim to be the top agent in the world. With the stress of making sure his agents and his team are successful by way of education, research, hard work and specialized knowledge, Ahmad truly wants to see his agents grow and prosper along with the company. With a widespread background and knowledge in the local Real Estate market in Toronto, Ahmad is dedicated taking his business to the very top. As being a proud member of the exclusive accredited platinum real estate professional Craig Proctor coaching member which only includes 200 members, Ahmad has the right team and support to guarantee success in every area of his business.

Myranda Shields

Myranda Shields is an owner of Horizon Southwest Realty. She has been in the real estate industry since 2004, when she graduated from ASU with a bachelor's degree in marketing. Myranda completed large scale statistical analysis projects for large companies and has an in-depth working knowledge of buyer behavior. She implements the most up-to-date technology in her business and creates a personal marketing plan for each client, then uses several different metrics to monitor the progress of that plan. Her honest and open approach keeps her clients aware of every detail of their transaction. She understands the stresses that moving puts on a family and works flexible hours to accommodate her clients schedules. Throughout her impressive career she has closed thousands of transactions and has a working knowledge in every area of residential real estate.

Myranda is well respected in the real estate community and as a Realtor ® who grew up in the Phoenix, AZ area, her relationships with industry professionals run deep. She puts these relationships to work for her clients in every transaction and applies her expertise and knowledge to help clients navigate the complex buying and selling process while positioning them for success.

www.ingramcontent.com/pod-product-compliance
Lightning Source LLC
Chambersburg PA
CBHW030905180526
45163CB00004B/1713